DYING WE LIVE

Meditations for Lent and Easter

EUGEN DREWERMANN

Edited by Linda M. Maloney

Translation by Linda M. Maloney

and John Drury

ORBIS BOOKS

Maryknoll, New York 10545

The Catholic Foreign Mission Society of America (Maryknoll) recruits and trains people for overseas missionary service. Through Orbis Books, Maryknoll aims to foster the international dialogue that is essential to mission. The books published, however, reflect the opinions of their authors and are not the official position of the society.

Translated from the German *Leben, das dem Tod entwächst: Predigten zur Passions—und Osterzeit,* by Eugen Drewermann, published by Patmos Verlag, Düsseldorf © 1991.

English translation edited by Linda M. Maloney, translated by Linda M. Maloney and John Drury, copyright © 1994 by Orbis Books.

Scripture citations taken from the *New American Bible with Revised New Testament* © 1969, 1970, and 1986, Confraternity of Christian Doctrine, used with permission.

Library of Congress Cataloging-in-Publication Data

Drewermann, Eugen.
   [Leben, das dem Tod entwächst. English]
   Dying we live : meditations for Lent and Easter / Eugen Drewermann ;
   edited by Linda M. Maloney ; translated by Linda M. Maloney and
John Drury.
      p.   cm.
   Translation of: Leben, das dem Tod entwächst.
   ISBN 0-88344-855-6
   1. Paschal mystery—Sermons.   2. Catholic Church—Sermons.
3. Sermons, English.   I. Maloney, Linda M.   II. Title.
BV55.D7413   1994
252' .6—dc20   93-36665
                                           CIP

Contents

First Week of Lent

1. What Makes Human Beings Wicked?

Now the serpent was the most cunning of all the animals that the Lord God had made. The serpent asked the woman: "Did God really tell you not to eat from any of the trees in the garden?" The woman answered the serpent: "We may eat of the fruit of the trees in the garden; it is only about the fruit of the tree in the middle of the garden that God said, 'You shall not eat it or even touch it, lest you die.' " But the serpent said to the woman: "You certainly will not die! No, God knows well that the moment you eat of it your eyes will be opened and you will be like gods who know what is good and what is bad." The woman saw that the tree was good for food, pleasing to the eyes, and desirable for gaining wisdom. So she took some of its fruit and ate it; and she also gave some to her husband, who was with her, and he ate it. Then the eyes of both of them were opened, and they realized that they were naked; so they sewed fig leaves together and made loincloths for themselves (Gn 3: 1-7).

What makes human beings wicked? This question is posed on the first page of the Bible, and it is one of the most anguishing questions we may ask ourselves when we have trouble understanding our own heart or when the cunning and wickedness of others makes us feel like giving up or ending it all.

The primeval stories and origin myths of earth's peoples are devoted to this puzzle, and they never mean to tell us about something past and gone. They are concerned with the process that takes hold of a human being whenever he or she falls into evil. It was so in primeval times because it always was and always will be so. The Bible tells us that the world is not the problem. It was created by God, and for human beings it could be a paradise, a garden, in which they were destined to be happy. Everything in nature is grand and wisely made, if only we human beings were willing to seek out our own true measure and goal.

How is it possible that human beings manage to go against the source of their own existence and the wellspring of their happiness? Whence comes the wall of separation that has arisen between God and humanity? Whence come the fences and the barbed wire human beings use to protect themselves from each other? And what forces upon us the locks and bolts that keep our thoughts and feelings separated from each other? The common teaching about human guilt and sin suggests that we all could be a little bit better if only we truly wanted to be. That is true, and no one would deny it. But it does not explain the uncanny energy and power of evil. We certainly could be a little bit better. The puzzling question is: Why are we so often trapped in the prison of evil? Or, to be more honest and accurate: Why, in some sense, are we perpetually trapped in the bonds of evil? The common teaching is that we human beings have an inclination to guilt and sin that is rooted in pride and disobedience. God is pictured as a wise lawgiver. We needed only to keep God's commandments to live happily and be at peace with ourselves.

How clear the commandments of God can be to a human being is a moot question. But if God has something crucial and essential to say to human beings, and if they are capable of sensing it in the very depths of their being and existence, whence comes the impulse to go against these all-wise and all-good words of the power to which we owe our existence? Human beings can be disobedient if they do not understand orders, if their dignity is insulted, if they feel oppressed and want to assert their rights against a dictatorial will. Disobedience can be productive and valuable. But such simple human notions definitely do not explain what prompts us human beings to go against God. We know proud human beings, and we can feel pride in ourselves. But we can never help but notice as well how much we distrust ourselves deep down, how unsure of ourselves we are, and how close we are to self-contempt whenever we feel we have to pretend to be more than we are in front of others. Pride is not a pristine way of feeling or acting. It is a reaction to feelings of inferiority. The common teaching about human sinfulness offers us no answer. We must bid adieu to all the practical theories that would have us believe we need only reflect a bit, muster our will, repent of this or that action, make reparation, and everything will be all right.

Sin is a fearsome thing, at least as the Bible describes it. It is brought to human beings by the most mysterious creature of mythology, the serpent. This creature is a superb intelligence to whom human beings fall prey without even realizing it right away. If you want to understand anything at all about the problem of evil, suggests the writer to whom we are indebted for the account of the Fall, then forget the notion that sin was produced by ill will. That is only superficially correct, if at all. If you want to understand the problem of evil, then you must see human beings as creatures who have been outwitted and seduced. They are the victims of a temptation to believe that this is their only road to good fortune and happiness, and only when it is far too late do they realize that what awaits them at the end of that road is sheer misfortune.

The serpent was more cunning than any other creature made by God. Even before the curtain rises, this little hint is given to explain the whole tragedy that follows. The first attempt to outwit human beings, to drive a wedge between God and humanity, comes from the serpent. We hear it ask a question that sounds quite harmless, inquiring about what God had said: "Did God really tell you not to eat from any of the trees in the garden?" Could there be a more fanciful or fantastic beginning for a temptation than inquiring about something that God had said? Could there be a nicer question than one asking about the words of God? The only catch is that the serpents question calls God into question. It foists on God a line of talk that is wholly alien to God. But it is possible to think along those lines. Did God make the whole world chock-full of happy possibilities to serve human beings in their quest for joy and good luck, only to keep them out of our reach by forbidding them to us? This is the first time anyone raises a question about God; and if we were to participate in a poll today concerning what we think about God, we might well answer a hearty yes to the question. There is no doubt that we experience God in that way. God has created a whole world, and it would be a beautiful one in and for itself except for the fact that everything nice is sinful. If that is correct, or if we take it to be correct, then we get what we today call religion: We struggle to be true to God—against our will, gnashing our teeth, and suspecting all the while that to fight on God's side means to lose out on the happy possibilities of this world.

Calling God into question, the serpent plays a wicked game. We feel for the human being, the woman, as we see her trying desperately to put God back in the right light. She makes clear that God did not say what the serpent had claimed, and she recalls what God did say. Word for word she reiterates God's commandment. We must realize and appreciate this, I think, if we want to understand why and how human beings sin. To say it again: If it were merely a matter of ill will, pride, and disobedience, then we could to some extent be meek, obedient, and good. The problem is that we human beings try desperately to be good and stay on the right road, to fight on God's side; but we can only do that under the sway of anxiety. For even as the woman reiterates God's commandment, she adds something that God did not say but that indicates what God's commandment means for her now: You shall not even touch the forbidden fruit, lest you die.

One single question from the serpent changes the whole image of God, hence of the world. Now it appears that God could descend like an avenging angel and execute the human being. Far removed now is any feeling that God gave a commandment simply to keep the human being safe in the circle of God's own joy. Now God, the very ground of our existence, becomes a hostile power, a human counterforce that produces anxiety. Woe to us if we do not keep God's commandments! God now shows up as a principle of death, a regent of despotic force. Now the woman feels anxiety about everything: anxiety about the tree in the garden; anxiety over herself, since she is capable of doing wrong; and anxiety about God, who has forbidden something. There is no place to stand that is not riddled with anxiety. Into this situation the serpent interjects its calming words of reassurance: "You certainly will not die!" That is precisely what she is waiting to hear so that the anxiety will go away. And the serpent adds a little explanation that is truly diabolical: We human beings shouldn't feel anxiety before God; rather, it is God who is afraid, and who laid down this prohibition just to keep human beings down. Despots are cruel when they fear those under them, and the severity of God's prohibition is merely an indication of hidden weakness.

When and if our religious piety becomes distorted and turns into sheer tyranny, then at some point human beings may be obligated to rid themselves of their God. At that point all the good fortune and happiness of the world coalesces around one single thing—the thing that is forbidden. There is no longer any pathway in paradise that does not lead us to the spot with the signpost: Do not touch. As soon as the serpent has taken the anxiety out of the woman's heart, this one tree with its fruit becomes the irresistible epitome of everything worth wanting and going after. As if hypnotized, she now reaches out for it—herself like God, herself a person of knowledge—so she hopes. The problem with us human beings is never that we do not get what we want. The problem of sin is that we do literally get what we go after, and it looks completely different. Almost as soon as we open our eyes, we notice what we ourselves are without God: mere dust, shamefully naked, helpless, exposed, impotent, worthless. God had good reason to deny the tree of knowledge to us, because the content of this knowledge—of what helps and harms us, what makes us happy and miserable—is good and evil in the moral sense. We should never have had to see what it means to have to live as creatures without our Creator; how in desperation a curse is born out of a blessing; and how we must begin to hate our ugly selves once the eyes of our Creator no longer gaze benevolently on our existence. Everything in the way of cramped necessity, deadly contradiction, and tormenting anguish arises out of our feeling of shame, our origin in dust, and our nakedness. We will perpetually fight against our pitiful state. Then there is room for pride and disobedience and haughtiness, for Promethean delusion and titanic striving. We are finally driven out, far from our standard and goal. We are the exiled children of Eve.

How we are redeemed from this trap that makes us wicked out of fear is something that the rest of the Bible will proceed to describe. God will accompany us on the long road of our history. God will try to take each one of us by the hand and tell us gently: You can find me again. The serpent is wrong. Do not believe the slanderer of God any more. Do not listen to those who tell you that the world is good but

God has forbidden it to you. Do not listen to those who whisper that God's commandments serve only to oppress you. God is your ally. God wanted you to be, and God is the only one who can ensure that you will reach the full measure of good fortune and happiness in a world where you can live safely. There is no longer any basis for wickedness when human beings find their way back to good fortune and happiness beyond anxiety.

2. How Do We Get to God?

God said to Noah and to his sons with him: "See, I am now establishing my covenant with you and your descendants after you, and with every living creature that was with you: all the birds, and the various tame and wild animals that were with you and came out of the ark. I will establish my covenant with you, that never again shall all bodily creatures be destroyed by the waters of a flood; there shall not be another flood to devastate the earth." God added: "This is the sign that I am giving for all ages to come, of the covenant between me and you and every living creature with you: I set my bow in the clouds to serve as a sign of the covenant between me and the earth. When I bring clouds over the earth, and the bow appears in the clouds, I will recall the covenant I have made between me and you and all living beings, so that the waters shall never again become a flood to destroy all mortal beings" (Gn 9:8-15).

How do we human beings get to God? There is one type of piety and spirituality in which God is seen as a higher principle of morality and ideal humanity. Brought up with such a conception of God, human beings can only strive with all their might to climb the ladder to heaven step by step and stage by stage, getting closer to God by virtue of their righteousness, perfection, and purity.

Right away, in the first few pages of the Bible, this way of worshiping God meets with fearful shipwreck. For if we start out by looking at the world and ourselves in terms of flawless righteousness and perfection, in terms of purity clear as glass, we soon realize that humanity is unworthy of its Creator. The feelings of guilt become more and more oppressive, the pressures of reparation and obligation become heavier and heavier, and the vicious circle becomes more and more inescapable. If you make up a completely pure, strict, and righteous God, then one day you are bound to attribute to that God what the myths of all peoples have repeatedly attributed to their gods. They tell us that one day the Creator looked at creation and stepped in, enraged with the sorry spectacle. No longer recognizing the divine image in creation, the Creator decided to wash away all the filth in the world, humanity in particular. To bring the world back to its pristine purity and cleanliness, God lets it rain until all living things are drowned in the ensuing deluge. It is a terrible image of punishment, but also of justifiable righteousness, for if we are a bit honest, we must admit that the thought is not wholly off base.

Who among us would still be alive if we were measured strictly by the yardstick of good and evil, true and false, clean and unclean, perfect and imperfect? Now, we could fool ourselves into thinking that we can do all right with such a standard. We need only make a little effort to do things right, and everything will turn out fine. But that is not correct. If we are courageous enough to look at the situation more closely, we soon notice that the middle-class order of average mediocrity cannot still the anxiety of our hearts. It is not enough to keep the laws and stipulations of that code in general. At some point we must ask ourselves about motives, feelings, and the unconscious underground of the soul. We then become increasingly stranger to ourselves, opening into the abyss.

For earnest and consistent human beings, such as Paul before Damascus, the balance sheet becomes increasingly somber and desperate. Paul had spent his whole life trying to be true to God by keeping the more than six hundred laws of the Old Testament. He found that it did not work—it simply did not work—even with the best will in the world. When the word of God is taken literally in its legal aspects, then the people of good will and earnest effort, the people who do not just skim over the surface of life, are precisely the ones who are driven to despair with almost clockwork regularity. That is the moment when people begin to understand the God who made the flood: a tidy solution to get a clean world. Once you start down that road, there can be no end to the cleaning out and overturning, no end to the ongoing process of destruction.

A modern play at one point has a man and woman trying to say something about the horrors of human history. In a rage, the man says: "Those guys should simply be exterminated. There should be a new flood to take care of them. Those that built the concentration camps and started wars, all those profligates, murderers, and obedient idiots— someone should let the rain pour down on them until they all float away." The woman asks, "And who, then, should be allowed to live?" The man replies, "The ones who should be permitted to live are the musicians, artists, writers—the good human beings." And the woman says, "But don't you realize that the people who ran the concentration camps spent their evenings listening to Beethoven and playing violins? They were no different; they were the very same people."

However horrible the world may seem, there is no pure or clean solution. So we must realize, says this biblical passage, that God is something more than a strict judge. Our lives can begin again when we are rooted in God, when we can cherish the thought that God will sustain us through all the vicissitudes of our lives and human history. We are permitted to exist, and we do exist, which proves that God is our ally, our covenant partner.

Since the time of the Flood, God apparently has given up the idea of ever seeing a pure world and a pure humanity. Instead, God would like to be better understood, to be more profoundly imitated in the ways of patience, understanding, and goodness. God makes a covenant with us and all creatures. It is the moment when God's whole creation seems to be knitted together. Only at this point in the Bible does the chasm between humanity and the rest of the animal world seem to be wiped out. Not only we ourselves, but also all our fellow creatures, are to be seen as covenant partners of God, and God is to be seen as the covenant partner of all created things.

That certainly has something to do with the way we treat ourselves. It means that we no longer have any good reason to repress or exterminate our untamed "animal" side. Perhaps it was not right for us simply to forget or suppress the millions of years of evolution during which humanity developed out of the animal kingdom; the process of becoming human goes on in the heart of every human being. Every human being needs patience, understanding, and kindness to grow more human day by day and to get closer to God. No one has the right to disown the warm and kindly power of the creation from which we have issued.

The other side of the coin is that we have no right or justifiable reason to act as tyrants or exploiters in our dealings with our fellow creatures. Since this is the only place in the Bible where human beings and animals are presented as covenant partners with each other and God, I want to take advantage of this unique opportunity to say something on this subject.

In an earlier day, the Church used the beginning of Lent to get people to reduce their intake of food, of meat in particular. On the First Sunday of Lent, it spelled out in detail what could be eaten, when, and how much, seeing fast and abstinence as ways for people to purify themselves. I think we have good reason to do some thinking about this whole matter, to reconsider the way we live and deal with our fellow creatures. It is a point, I think, that Christianity has tended to pass over in silence. Yet it also offers us a solid basis not so much for observing Lent as for living with the creatures around us in a more benevolent way.

I suspect that almost all of us have been touched at some point in our lives by a house pet or farm animal: the sleek and supple cat, the loyal watchdog, the proud rooster, the canary songster. We all love animals, of course. Yet we are the same people who take no notice of the fact that millions of animals are systematically killed in gruesome ways to stock our table. They are part of the food chain for us, produced, processed, and delivered fresh and appetizing to us. That has become so normal for us that we do not even see a problem with it. But there is a big problem: Animals are God's covenant partners, and they do not deserve to be treated like that by us.

Some may say, "That's a lot of nonsense. If you have a dog, you know it eats meat. So why shouldn't we human beings?" Well, precisely because we are human beings, not dogs. We can take time out to reflect, which other animals cannot do. We are not just part of the food chain, thank God. We are capable of being more humane in our dealings with animals, and I think we should be, on human grounds, first of all. Every kilogram of meat costs seven kilograms of animal feed, which is produced largely in countries of the Third World. We import that feed, that food, only to fatten animals who will eventually tickle our own taste buds. It is difficult to change eating habits, but there is often good reason to correct mistaken behavior.

Compassion is the other reason for more humane dealings with animals. It is a finer thing to let animals live than to kill them. George Bernard Shaw may have been right when he said that some day, hopefully soon, the eating of animals would be considered as barbaric as the eating of human beings. Then Christianity will be asked why it did not say that sooner; why it did not point to God's covenant with Noah and make clear that plants, birds, and all animals are covenant partners with God, and that we, too, should be on God's side and be kind to all creatures.

There is a marvelous passage in Psalm 104 where the psalmist notes that God created Leviathan simply to sport in the sea and take its delight in it (Ps 104:26). The same can be said of all the animals in this world. I can't believe that God is pleased when we brutalize and kill animals as a matter of course, for no other reason than that it suits us. That does not make us better human beings. On the contrary, it only makes us more dull witted, thoughtless, and brutal. A child would be shocked to see what we adults take for granted. What keeps us from giving up that behavior and becoming truly adult? The goodness of God is universal, and we all can inject a bit of it into our own lives. What the Church once proposed as an exceptional counsel for achieving personal perfection can become a better way of relating to ourselves and all the creatures around us. Then God's promise for all of history becomes a reality. Anxiety and melancholy may often gather in our own hearts, as clouds do in the sky, but we need only look to see the light of God amid the darkness, splintering into all the colors of the rainbow to give us hope. Never again on earth will destruction, cruelty, and condemnation have the last word. Instead we must try to grow together in the goodness of God.

3. Confession—Sin—Risk

"It will be as when a man who was going on a journey called in his servants and entrusted his possessions to them. To one he gave five talents; to another, two; to a third, one—to each according to his ability. Then he went away. Immediately the one

*who received five talents went and traded with them, and made
another five. Likewise, the one who received two made another
two. But the one who received one went off and dug a hole in the
ground and buried his master's money. After a long time the
master of those servants came back and settled accounts with
them. The one who had received five talents came forward
bringing the additional five. He said, 'Master, you gave me five
talents. See, I have made five more.' The master said to the
servant: 'Well done, my good and faithful servant. Since you
were faithful in small matters, I will give you great responsibilities. Come, share your master's joy.' [Then] the one who had
received two talents also came forward and said: 'Master, you
gave me two talents. See, I have made two more.' His master said
to him: 'Well done, my good and faithful servant. Since you were
faithful in small matters, I will give you great responsibilities.
Come, share your master's joy.' Then the one who had received
the one talent came forward and said, 'Master, I knew you were
a demanding person, harvesting where you did not plant and
gathering where you did not scatter; so out of fear I went off and
buried your talent in the ground. Here it is back.' His master said
to him in reply: 'You wicked, lazy servant! So you knew that I
harvest where I did not plant and gather where I did not scatter?
Should you not then have put my money in the bank so that I
could have got it back with interest on my return? Now then! Take
the talent from him and give it to the one with ten. For to everyone
who has, more will be given and he will grow rich; but from the
one who has not, even what he has will be taken away. And throw
this useless servant into the darkness outside, where there will
be wailing and grinding of teeth' " (Mt 25:14-30).*

At the beginning of Lent, the Church regularly urges its faithful to
receive the sacrament of Reconciliation and laments the fact that
ever-increasing numbers of them are not making sufficient use of this
important sacrament and its offer of God's grace. Now the fact is that
the institution of Confession is a good and useful thing in a real sense.
There is no doubt that at certain times and intervals we need to evaluate
ourselves and see where we are. There is a real advantage in being
assured, in God's name, that nothing can separate us from God's
forgiveness and grace in a definitive way. With a little good will, we

need never succumb to feelings of ultimate anxiety or despair, to feelings that all is lost. Why, then, are so many people so terribly afraid to enter the confessional and receive the sacrament of Reconciliation?

Many people have gone to Confession since childhood and feel more or less comfortable with it. What I am going to say now will be of little or no use to them. But there are others, indeed a growing majority, who have had problems with Confession since childhood. They gave it up a long time ago and no longer care whether their children stick to it after the age of fourteen. It is to them, in particular, that I would like to address a few words. It seems to me that this discomfort with an important sacrament of the Church must contain some element of truth that deserves to be recognized and appreciated. Perhaps it embodies some rightful claim that the Church has chosen to evade for centuries rather than to satisfy. The Church now complains that at times of crisis many would rather see a psychologist or therapist in an office than a priest in the confessional. But if that is the case for many, if they can spend an hour with a therapist and purchase understanding for a fee, what conclusion are we to draw about Confession?

If we look at the matter more closely, I think we will find at least three things that we in the Catholic Church have to learn from psychology, whether we like it or not.

First, there is something we could have learned from Jesus' own teaching two thousand years ago. It is a part of our faith's teaching about Reconciliation, and we must take it to heart today. It tells us that no one can receive the sacrament of Reconciliation who has not already been reborn through the grace of Baptism and received a new life through this rebirth in Christ. If we take this seriously, then it means that we cannot even practice truthfulness or make an honest evaluation of our situation in life unless we have learned to trust that there is forgiveness for us in every circumstance of life and death. That is no small or trifling matter.

On the other hand, we have been thoroughly taught that we can and should feel accepted when we are in harmony with certain laws and norms; but if we deviate from them, we must fear punishment. Indeed, in the Church there is a clear distinction between venial and mortal sins. The former we need only confess to God, and God will forgive us. The latter will condemn us to hell if we do not get absolution from a duly authorized priest. With these teachings in the back of our mind, we go through life examining and censuring ourselves far into the night. We are riddled with anxiety, and so we put on masks in our dealings with others and even with ourselves. We are careful to keep a veil over the shadowy corners of our lives, and so we never even get in touch with ourselves, though we may have the best intentions in the world.

Here is where we can learn something from modern psychology. It can take years for a human being to be able to grasp a little more truth about himself or herself, and that is basically what Jesus wanted. He felt very close to the hundredth sheep in the flock, to the people who were despised by society as prostitutes, thieves, and tax collectors. Such people could no longer wear any masks. Their lives were lived on the edge and so splintered that there was no longer any good reason for them to indulge in pretense. Beyond a certain point, shame and hypocritical poses have no place. People have no energy left to keep up the lie. Jesus saw that these people knew very well that in the end we are totally dependent on God's mercy. He felt close to them and comfortable in their presence, more at home with them than with the ninety-nine sheep who, he said, had no need of conversion.

But what are we to make of the fact that today 90 percent of the faithful will not take one step toward the sacrament of Reconciliation? Is it possible that they no longer have any confidence that there is room in the Church for forgiveness without criticism, accusation, and summary condemnation? But that is the sort of space that Jesus wanted. He wanted the Temple to open its doors to these lost souls. He wanted us to be free of anxiety and full of trust when we speak of God, because only that could truly change our lives.

Second, if we take that seriously, then we must realize that it is much more important to consider people's motives than to judge their actions in terms of some hard and fast rule. The Catholic Church has been big on spelling out the difference between venial and mortal sins in a given area of conduct. It was not so long ago that the Church could pinpoint exactly the start of mortal sin when a person was watching a movie, or when a teenage boy and a teenage girl were sitting together on a park bench. This precise knowledge about going to hell has condemned the Church in the view of the poetry, the feelings, the sensitivities, and the honesty of whole generations raised within the Church, and it may take decades or centuries for that guilt to be erased. It has filled people with anxiety rather than confidence, with self-hatred and a lack of daring in the face of life, and it has done this in the name of God, who sees everything and who can peer where no human being can.

For the generation now growing up, the Church's power to generate such guilt feelings has evaporated to a large extent, and interest in Confession has faded proportionately. But the same people have a keen feeling for what is right and what is not right. Instead of learning fixed, inflexible norms in school, they are learning how to speak to one another in ways that are fair and that give the other person a chance to keep the channels of communication open in areas of conflict. This basic attitude and approach to dialogue, which permits other people to say what they mean, is what we call "democracy" as a fundamental way of life and community. Their feelings and intended meanings are far more important than what simply takes place as a concrete action. It is the tone that makes the human being.

Thus all life's questions become much more complicated. It simply is not possible to determine what is right or good by looking at externals. Everything floats in ambiguity, and life is a more dialectical process. So it was with Jesus of Nazareth. If we theologians want to turn our noses up at psychologists, we must realize that Jesus is the standard by which we are to gauge our own conduct. One day he had accepted an invitation from a group of good people among the Pharisees. While he was with them, a prostitute dared to approach him, this man of God. She threw herself at his feet, weeping, while his worthy hosts waited to see how he would deal with such trash and preserve his dignity as a man of God. When he looked into the face of the unfortunate woman, however, Jesus did not see sinfulness, but a boundless longing for love. As his astonished audience looked on, he assured her that God had forgiven her. The world is completely changed when we look at the hearts of human beings rather than their hands, and John's Gospel tells us that Jesus knew what was *in* human beings.

Third, we must realize that certain things may be true and correct at one point in a person's life but incorrect at another point. The confessional guide with which we grew up contains a whole series of rules for adults that would be grotesque if applied equally to a teenager or a preteen. By the same token, certain norms can have some meaning when we are still children and cannot figure things out for ourselves. To be obedient and to avoid nibbling things are sensible dictates when we cannot yet distinguish between sweets and poisonous substances. But when we are capable of personal insight and judgment, when we have a right to claim what we need, then strict, unquestioning obedience may become a barrier to life itself. The same is true for many other things.

Another situation is much more difficult. There are things that are undeniably wrong according to the laws of morality, yet some people do them and, up to this point in their lives, *cannot* feel repentance for them. The actions seem so necessary, so much a part of their lives. Psychology can teach us that people caught in temptation and error need to find that little dose of truth that is meant for their lives. It can also teach us that if some things are forbidden too early in life, people may have to learn them later. Don't we in the Church bear a heavy burden of blame for expecting people to be perfect experts in the most important areas of human life? Consider the whole issue of love and lovemaking. Before marriage it is sinful; in marriage it is a duty; outside of marriage it is again sinful. It is all simple and clear-cut. But when do people under such pressure learn to love and to dream? And how can they suddenly move from lovemaking as sin to lovemaking as a duty without feeling anger or hatred for themselves or ultimately for the person who is living by their side?

There are so many problems we have not dared even to mention, much less acknowledge and deal with, and they only get worse when we go and bar the door to them in the name of morality. One of Jesus' most important instructions in the Sermon on the Mount was that if a person forces you to go one mile with him or her, you should go two. He was trying to tell us that what people need is accompaniment through thick and thin, wherever it may lead. It is a matter of taking our place by the side of others when they are suffering from anxiety. It is not a matter of pushing our way into their lives obtrusively, already knowing what has to be corrected. They themselves know that.

We fall into error frequently, but, as God sees it, there are certain things we should realize and believe. Insofar as God is concerned, not only can we obtain forgiveness when we do wrong, but we also have a right to make mistakes when we mean well. In the end there really is no clear and universally valid order of good and evil, virtue and vice. Instead there is "a sound of sheer silence" (1 Kgs 19:12) in our hearts, a feeling for what is human, and a touch of compassion for everything living on this earth. In the end there is only one sin in God's eyes, which is made clear in this parable of the talents: To bury everything and refuse to risk our lives out of sheer anxiety, perhaps even before God. But that is not the God of Jesus Christ, and it should not be the God we worship in the Church.

4. *Facing Temptation*

Filled with the Holy Spirit, Jesus returned from the Jordan and was led by the Spirit into the desert for forty days, to be tempted by the devil. He ate nothing during those days, and when they were over he was hungry. The devil said to him: "If you are the Son of God, command this stone to become bread." Jesus answered him: "It is written, 'One does not live by bread alone.'" Then he took him up and showed him all the kingdoms of the world in a single instant. The devil said to him: "I shall give to you all this power and their glory; for it has been handed over to me, and I may give it to whomever I wish. All this will be yours, if you worship me." Jesus said to him in reply: "It is written, 'You shall worship the Lord, your God, and him alone shall you serve.'" Then he led him to Jerusalem, made him stand on the parapet of the temple, and said to him: "If you are the Son of God, throw yourself down from here, for it is written, 'He will command his angels concerning you, to guard you' and 'With their hands they will support you, lest you dash your foot against a stone.'" Jesus said to him in reply: "It also says, 'You shall not put the Lord, your God, to the test.'" When the devil had finished every temptation, he departed from him for a time (Lk 4:1-13).

What a person understands by temptation will ultimately depend on his or her personal experience of external dangers and internal threats. Martin Scorsese's film of the Kazantzakis novel *The Last Temptation of Christ* prompted much discussion about the possibility of Jesus being tempted, in the face of death, to seek happiness on earth by the side of Mary Magdalene and to live a quiet domestic life. The mere possibility, suggested near the end of the film, was enough to evoke moral condemnation of the movie. It evoked the image of a Jesus who might have believed that the kingdom of God would begin when the human heart and the earth became one. People apparently felt anxiety that the breaking of a taboo would bring down the wall of separation between the holy and the sinful, between the pure man of God and the impure prostitute. Our Catholic religious consciousness apparently draws great strength from that wall of separation. But in the case of Jesus of Nazareth, do we really have good reasons to fear love and to scorn earthly domesticity? Is this what Jesus really wanted, but something we who call ourselves Christians feel we have to run away from: the idea that this earthly life rests in the hands of God without fear or division? Must we practice a neurotic Christianity to protect ourselves from the real Jesus? Must we encase our anxieties in absurd moral formulas, thinking all the while that Jesus wanted it that way?

Luke's account of Jesus' temptations is about something very different. It is not the tempting of a human being who is uncomfortable with himself, who is suffering so much from inner conflicts and turmoil that whole parts of his soul are prey to the devil. The temptations here have to do with this world. To be sure, the account and its external images make things simpler than they are in reality. When we read the story, it is immediately clear to us that the devil is the one speaking to Jesus. He cites the word of God, the prayer book of Israel, and proves to be conversant with Scripture. Jesus' temptation, in other words, is not something external but a matter of toying with possibilities that stem from the religious sphere itself, from God's command, and the question is how one understands the matter.

It may be true in a superficial way to say that Jesus is tempted by his own hunger to turn stones into bread. In his own life he certainly experienced all human needs. But in this case it is not a matter of eating his fill this one time. What kind of a temptation would that be? A whole principle of life is at stake here, a whole program for the redemption of the world. Before Jesus steps out in public and utters a single word to human beings, he himself must know what he will speak to them about, what need affects them most deeply. We need only open our eyes to see and hear the boundless, shrieking misery around us, to be prompted to ask not only how God can permit it, but also how in God's name we can do something to counter it all. Is it not the first and most fundamental fact of **human** existence that we are creatures who feel hunger? Biology tells **us** that life is basically nothing but metabolism. If we go just a couple of days without the right mix of basic nourishment, we find all our good thoughts and resolutions fading from our mind. It is impossible to talk about God or high ideals to people whose intestines are suffering hunger pangs. The first duty of compassion is to combat the depletion of human beings by unjust suffering and loss of basic energy. People of the past two centuries may well appreciate this particular temptation in the desert more clearly than the people of Jesus' own day could. Given the growing catastrophe of hunger and starvation in the world in our own time, religion today is compelled to speak first of nothing else but human suffering and the compassion that God wants us to show.

But are human beings essentially creatures who can be satisfied with food? Do we really help them when we stop there? The paradox is that we must see human beings as creatures greater than their need if we want to find some basis for getting beyond the suffocating pall of egoism. If it is true that human beings live by food and nothing more, then the battle over resources will never cease and our horizon will never expand enough to take in all human beings. We must see humanity as greater than that if we want to be able to help human beings when they are down. Humanity does not live by bread alone. We often latch on to external things as substitutes for what we really need. It is frequently the case that the emptier we are inside, the more we feel a need for food, clothing, money, and a comfortable livelihood. We may even feel the deprivation of hunger most keenly when everything seems to be all right on the outside, and one day we may feel the poverty of our soul even more keenly than the poverty of our body. The hunger of human beings must be satisfied in its endless yearning, and the belly, for all its intrinsic worth, is almost nothing but a symbol of that yearning. //

At this point, all we need do is quote the Bible, and it again becomes contradictory and dialectical. If it is possible to imagine the sort of greatness human beings can possess, then we are immediately faced with the question of how one is to deal with them. We need only peruse the course of human history to see that it is a graveyard of contradictions, conflicts, rapes, and bloody battles. How, then, may one establish peace and justice on this earth? The temptation of Jesus to seize power is not to be viewed as an attempt to increase his own self-importance by winning crown and scepter. But look at the world around us: If some people have the personal strength, do they not also have a duty to take power in order to wield it *in favor of* human beings for a change instead of *against* them, as usually happens? Mustn't we care that the *right* people take over the important positions sometimes, instead of letting them fall into the hands of the arrogant and power hungry, who climb over corpses to get to the top? The temptation to seize power would have faced Jesus every day if he focused his attention on the military might of Rome and its barbaric actions in the province of Judea. It caused much suffering for the peasants, it installed its own puppets to squeeze money from the people, and it acted as if it were God. Knowing what God could be, wouldn't Israelites feel driven to a holy rebellion against such behavior?

In an awesome moment, Jesus looks at the kingdoms of the world from a mountain top and learns that it is not possible to wield power without serving the devil. I do not see how any political theology can get around that. There is no question that we serve humanity when we get politically involved. There is no question that we have a duty to sweep things clean, insofar as we are able. But in principle one must know what one is about when the issue at hand is the redemption of humanity. The fairest government possible only brings people the return of their old problems, since they will not let themselves be governed like sheep, and the wisest order still does violence to them because they are human beings. It is not possible to force equality on human beings, to level them off like the grass in the field; they want to live with their differences. It may well be that government is necessary to establish a certain framework of external order; but then all the difficulties of human beings begin again, first and foremost the anxiety they feel in their hearts. The spiral of temptation starts all over. On the deepest need of human existence, we get no solid information or answers from biology or sociology, from the nutritional or the governmental sphere.

But what if we could organize religion, our talk about God, in such a way that no human being would any longer feel even a twinge of anxiety? Don't all of us wish some time or other that we could just let ourselves go once and for all? And isn't that what we hope and expect from God: to find rest and to be able to sink into God's open arms everywhere in this world? We really feel a need for a religion that would answer all of humanity's questions and leave none unanswered, that would still its fearful doubts with clear and certain answers. Religion is supposed to quiet the enduring uneasiness of human beings once and for all, showing God to be the immutable and eternally unchangeable one. What was valid a thousand years ago would still be valid a thousand years from now, and human certainty and security would find its guarantee in what religion had to say about God.

Insofar as Jesus of Nazareth is concerned, the question is how religion understands him. With all his being and all his actions, he clearly wanted to teach us trust in God and nothing else. But his trust in God took a curious form indeed. He walked on water dry shod and tried to teach us that we could stride above the abyss with our eyes fixed on the opposite shore. In this picture there is no stilling of anxiety. We can still hear the howling wind, we can still see the storm-tossed waters; but now we can cross over the narrow horizon of anxiety. Jesus of Nazareth wanted to teach us trust in God, and the diabolical temptation facing religion is to turn what he wanted into something completely different: into a system that turns God into something clearly known and understood once and for all. We then would no longer have a need for trust in God. We would need only the certainty of explanations about God on the lips of God's appointed servants. The depths of the abyss would bother us no more, and we would know everything about God because we had managed to avoid God. Wouldn't human beings really be helped if God were neatly wrapped in a little box that would make everyone feel secure?

Because of its crusades and inquisitions, the Catholic Church has often been described as intolerant, fanatic, power hungry, and cruel. Now all that may be true, but a certain kind of compassion may be the worst temptation of all. In the face of human hunger, we may wish for nothing more than that people at last get their fill of food. In the face of the glaring injustice of this world, we may wish to take up arms and indulge in a bloodbath until peace is established at last. In the case of religion, we may wish to compress it into a nice little house where everyone can live. But all that merely diminishes human beings, turns them into herd animals or tame rabbits, things that follow orders. It does not allow them to live as human beings, and it does not serve God, but the devil.

I often think that the devil is not the devil but a force with so much compassion for the suffering in this world that we no longer can bear the grandeur of the challenge, no longer can endure this world that we know in all its terror—free, open, unfolding, always in the process of being devoured and bringing itself to new birth. Then the word of God, with its talk about love, redemption, and trust, begins to be something very different that turns against human beings and against God. It is terribly difficult to differentiate between the two. Indeed, it is an ever-recurring battle that never comes to an end. In today's Gospel, the battle seems to be over, but Luke makes it clear that the devil will be back. We will encounter Jesus later at his last supper with his disciples, where he will celebrate the first Eucharist, and the questions will be the same: about food and sword and religion. Jesus' life is almost at an end. Everything to be said has been said. But was it enough? And what do we as Church make out of it? The same questions will dog us over the centuries, and we will either pass over the waters or founder, sinking deepest when we wish that the water had floorboards.

Second Sunday of Lent

5. Being a Blessing

The Lord said to Abram: "Go forth from the land of your kinsfolk and from your father's house to a land that I will show you. I will make of you a great nation, and I will bless you; I will make your name great, so that you will be a blessing. I will bless those who bless you and curse those who curse you. All the communities of the earth shall find blessing in you" (Gn 12:1-4).

The history of Israel, the history of salvation, begins with God's choosing of Abraham. For the first time, a glimmer of hope shines on the dark curtain. It is said that Abraham was called by God to leave Ur of the Chaldees in order to break away from the worship of other gods, but this biblical text tells us nothing of that. It is said that Abraham was chosen to found a great people. That is true, so long as we do not interpret it falsely in terms of a national ideology.

It is curious that when God calls him, Abraham really knows only one thing about his future: he will be great and a blessing for all. We can understand this contrast only if we consider what it would mean to be a human being without this choice of Abraham.

This is the first time in human history that God turns again to us and offers to take us beyond the primeval curse, to bring us back to a lost paradise where we can feel accepted and welcomed by God. During the whole of the time between the Fall and the call of Abraham, our normal human life seems to be played out in a dungeon of terrible sensations. We feel hunted and driven out, and we almost want to curse our own life. We are so filled with feelings of self-disgust and self-hatred that we can hardly impute any good to ourselves on this earth, and if we feel that way about ourselves, then we are sure that everyone else must have reason to feel the same way.

How do we human beings find our way back to the roots of trust that will enable us to live? Our lives are spent in an endless round of competition, an ongoing struggle to force the other's back to the wall. That is no life at all. From the slaying of Abel by Cain to the tower of Babel, everyone seeks to win back God's favor by following some formula: If you work very hard, if you are productive, if you are good, if you are successful, and if you then offer all that up to some horrendous god, perhaps someone will love you. They will love you for your anguish, for your penances, for your self-oppression. Perhaps if you exhaust yourself to the point where you can do no more, some god will have mercy on you. But alongside you are your brothers and sisters, and perhaps they are in better shape, hence a mortal danger to you.

What else can we do, then, but try to storm heaven, to become greater and greater, to pile up the earth under our feet until we manage to become gods ourselves, exercising power and guaranteeing our influence? If that means living in a world of false gods, of antihuman gods and inhuman behavior, then it is true that Abraham had to leave everything that had been familiar. The country in which he had lived his life was devastating his soul. Away, then, from his homeland, for it was his prison, the place where he did not feel at home at all. Away, then, from his father's house, for staying there meant crouching under the sway of human fear, bowing before the portrait of other people who acted as if they could treat you like a child forever: Do this, don't do that; here I am the boss, the father, the sham god, the bogey. So it is time to get away from your father's house and your homeland, to break the spell of human idols, the despotic dictates of human anxiety, the reign of ghosts.

For the first time since the beginning, in the time before human history, God again addresses a human being. Up to this point God spoke only to God, and people to each other, and every dialogue collapsed in mutual enmity. Here once again a human being hears what God has to say to all of us. We again catch a glimmer of our greatness, hear a promise of our true vocation. Abraham has nothing of his own, nothing to show. It is himself, his person, that counts.

At this turning point in human history there is really only one thing that God would like to say, but with all the force and emphasis to be found in God's own word. If we hear a voice within us and can be sure it comes from God, then we are faced with an inner necessity, an unavoidable dictate designed to preserve our worth and broaden our existence. The message given to Abraham is: You will be a blessing. Or, since future and present are not to be differentiated in this divine message: You, Abraham, are a blessing.

If it were not evident every day and everywhere that human beings, no matter how much they may talk about God, have a much stronger feeling that they are a burden and a curse to others, that their presence is too much to take, that it would be better if they did not even exist, then one might not understand why a whole world changes with this particular divine message. Now we are to think of ourselves as a blessing. Indeed, we have a sacred duty before God to see our lives as a blessing. We must recapture the feeling of being happy and grateful for our existence. We must feel that our existence enriches others, bringing good fortune, joy, and beauty into their lives.

Henceforth there is only one thing that God does not want and opposes one last time, as a warning to us: If anyone should dare to confront another human being with the words, "I curse you," the one who curses will invite God's rejection. Nothing will change if anxiety, hatred, and doubt continue. Paradise will remain infinitely far away.

What begins here with Abraham is to be the basis of all history. This small beginning is to change the world, because God will accompany us through history.

6. Changing Our Lives

He went around to the villages in the vicinity teaching. He summoned the Twelve and began to send them out two by two and gave them authority over unclean spirits. He instructed them to take nothing for the journey but a walking stick—no food, no sack, no money in their belts. They were, however, to wear sandals but not a second tunic. He said to them: "Wherever you enter a house, stay there until you leave from there. Whatever place does not welcome you or listen to you, leave there and shake the dust off your feet in testimony against them." So they went off and preached repentance. They drove out many demons, and they anointed with oil many who were sick and cured them (Mk 6:6b-13).

During these days we prepare to celebrate the death and resurrection of our savior, Jesus Christ, and we are supposed to devote ourselves to conversion, to changing our lives. When we hear these words, we think we know what they mean. Turning our lives around means turning away from sin. Sin is any offense against the commandments that God handed down on Sinai, that are inscribed in the law of the Old and New Testaments, and that are interpreted and explained by the Church. If we look at it that way, things are very simple. We need only do what we are supposed to do, and we can do that, if only we are willing to show a little good will.

As long as we see the world in this way, it remains more or less solid and well-ordered. But we repeatedly find ourselves in difficulty, struggling from one good resolution to another but repeatedly falling into a hole. It seems that as Jesus preached in the villages of Galilee, he felt drawn farther and farther away from the clear-cut guidelines and admonitions voiced by his teacher, John the Baptist. Apparently those who had gone astray or gotten lost could not come back simply because they would like to. There was so much in their hearts that drove them to the margins of life, and even more that held them there. Jesus must have felt very close to these particular human beings who did not have their lives in hand and who certainly could not change their way of living simply because they made a resolution to do so. As he sent his disciples out to preach conversion in the villages of Galilee, his use of the word took a curious turn. First of all, his disciples were to lay their hands on people and drive out demons. In Jesus' eyes it is as if our lives were taken over by a host of alien spirits and forces, as if we often had scarcely any control over ourselves, no matter how clear our thinking might be.

This impression seems to ring true again and again, when we look deeply enough. There is hardly any problem that admits of a purely moral solution. To put it another way, it seems that our clear-cut talk about good and evil is a foreshortening of human existence, a system of coercion that repeatedly proves helpless in the face of the actual problems of humanity. I remember very vividly an encounter I had with a man a few weeks after my ordination. It was just after Mass on a fine Sunday morning. He met me on the street, and he was in a state of utter bewilderment. During a brief stay in a medical facility, he had met a woman and fallen deeply in love with her. For more than twenty years he had been a happily married husband and a caring father—and now this. He felt that suddenly the basic underpinnings of his life had been washed away, as if by a flood. They seemed to have rotted out, to be incapable of sustaining him.

When one realizes that it can be this way in a human life, then the world is changed completely. It seems as if morality and its laws may be able to describe symptoms, but certainly not causes or the illness itself. In the eyes of Jesus, however, it is as if our whole life were an illness, something from which we suffer and with which we cannot deal on our own. What are we to do? Are we now to adopt the motto that necessity knows no law? Are we to accept the idea that divorce may be perfectly all right, that it does not really matter? No, not at all. But it may well matter, it may well be of some importance, that we consider and ponder what goes on in the human heart. Something that seems wrong from the outside may well be necessary, unavoidable, and right from the inside. We cannot simply stick to the outside, regarding human beings as somehow squeezed between moral dictates and concrete action. We must follow the trail of need into the depths and ask how a whole life has taken shape. Then all of us, without exception as Jesus sees it, will discover that throughout our lives we struggle to win love and recognition in some way, and we devote our all to that goal. We exert our best insights and efforts, and what happens? The more successful we are, the more people are drawn into our lives, and the greater our responsibility becomes. The farther we move along this road, the more we become the victims of decisions already made. It is as if we were on a stage, wearing costumes and masks so familiar that all others, and ultimately we ourselves, come to believe the role we are playing. In the end the role may take control of us, or we may be shipwrecked on ourselves, or an alien need may teach us the importance of being truthful. Whenever we reach our limits, conversion, "turning around," becomes inevitable. It was probably for that very reason that it was always the people who did not know how to go on or which way to turn who were drawn to Jesus and came to him.

About five hundred years before Christ, the sayings attributed to Lao Tzu succinctly expressed the predicament and its solution: When meaning is lost, so is life; when life is lost, so is love; when love is lost, so is righteousness; when righteousness is lost, so is conventional moral behavior. Morality is the absence of loyalty and faith and the beginning of complete confusion. Two examples were given. When good order in a family is destroyed, then people begin to talk about parental duty and the love of children. When the good order of a state is lost, then we get a host of efficient civil servants. The Chinese sages were trying to explain how human beings can find their way back to meaning in their lives and how they can learn to feel happy with their existence, so that love will flow naturally out of grateful satisfaction with the laws governing the world. Good behavior and morality would then come wholly from the inside. There is really only one sort of conversion, resulting not from compulsive willing but from a deep, inner trust in a gracious mercy that accompanies us and forgives us.

7. Seeing Who We Are

About eight days after he said this, he took Peter, John, and James and went up the mountain to pray. While he was praying, his face changed in appearance and his clothing became dazzling white. And behold, two men were conversing with him, Moses and Elijah, who appeared in glory and spoke of his exodus that he

*was going to accomplish in Jerusalem. Peter and his companions
had been overcome by sleep, but becoming fully awake, they saw
his glory and the two men standing with him. As they were about
to part from him, Peter said to Jesus: "Master, it is good that we
are here; let us make three tents, one for you, one for Moses, and
one for Elijah." But he did not know what he was saying. While
he was still speaking, a cloud came and cast a shadow over them,
and they became frightened when they entered the cloud. Then
from the cloud came a voice that said: "This is my chosen Son;
listen to him." After the voice had spoken, Jesus was found alone.
They fell silent and did not at that time tell anyone what they had
seen (Lk 9:28-36).*

What do we really know about the truth of a human being? He or
she may live by our side for years, and we may not notice anything
unusual about the person. But we cannot evaluate or judge a human
life by everyday events. There are times and moments in our lives when
everything we are is concentrated and hangs in the balance. At such
crucial moments it becomes very clear who we really are. It is not that
the truth of our person is really decided only at such moments. It is that
such times bring out clearly the vision and conviction that also shapes
our everyday life.

Undoubtedly, the decisive moment in Jesus' life was the one involv-
ing Gethsemane and Golgotha. For the early Church, however, this
moment makes clearer than ever what Jesus must have had before his
eyes all the time. The reality of Jesus was not that clear to his own
disciples. Their eyes were dimmed by anxiety and weariness of heart.
They could say nothing while Jesus was still with them. We cannot say
for sure that this gospel passage about Jesus' transfiguration came into
being after Easter. But isn't it true that we almost always grasp the truth
about a human being years later, while we were almost blind to it when
we were with the person?

What was the truth about Jesus, the truth for all time? This Gospel
tells us that we must ascend the mountain with Jesus if we wish to
understand him. To maintain the imagery, we can say that our lives are
lived in the lowlands and valleys. We seem to be thoroughly defined
by the laws of environment, inertia, and gravity. From this "lowland"
perspective, we appear to be puppets on a string, more acted upon than
actors. Such a life—nothing more than a clinging to earth—hardly

deserves to be called human. We are called to the heights, to greatness, and our soul is meant to take wings. We are intended to gather together everything in our being and life.

So Jesus takes the three disciples with him, leaves the plain, and literally goes up to a higher plane, where there is a broad view and eyes can see clearly. How does anyone climb such a mountain? We cannot look for it somewhere in space; the mountains of the heart are the upward sweeps of joy, experiences of absolute liberation, as if we had finally arrived at the very center of the world, or as if we had come to a sanctuary and left behind us everything that chokes and besieges and oppresses us. We human beings are called to touch the heavens with our foreheads and to hear the voice of God in our hearts.

In this Gospel the reality that is to be found in the life of Jesus and that shines forth from his figure for a moment is described in terms of two pillars of the Old Testament, Moses and Elijah. In Moses lives the vision of a freedom that led a whole people out of bondage and despotism, through the wilderness, into freedom. We human beings are not slaves of other human beings; we are free and responsible before God alone for our history. The prophet Elijah makes clear that God is not some gruesome idol and that there is no value to a religion based on anxiety-ridden demons. That was Elijah's message when he destroyed the Baals.

Freedom vis-à-vis human beings and trust in God are embodied in the figures of Moses and Elijah. They speak with Christ and come together in him; they are alive in him. For the early Church, it meant that however much new there was in the figure and message of Jesus, in him we also see the continuation of what was already present in the Old Covenant. Only we must understand how shockingly new the seemingly "old" often is and how much reaction it provokes in every age. Jesus himself tells the Israelites of his own day: You erect memorials to the prophets; but that only proves that you are the children of those who slew the prophets. People may appeal to the new and unexpected as if it were quite familiar, seeking thereby to squelch it.

Freedom vis-à-vis human beings and trust in God—how much anxiety is evoked when human beings begin to live that way, and how much sluggishness and weariness of heart must be stirred by disquiet if this is the true way of life. But it is *supposed* to be true and real. At the moment Jesus experiences it, it is immediately a pointer to Jerusalem and his death. It is true: Jesus needed Tabor to be able to endure

Golgotha. How much suffering a human being endures as the outcome of his or her own decisions rather than as an alien demand can be understood only in terms of that person's measure of happiness, clarity of truth, and powerful nearness to heaven.

It is impossible to fix such moments in writing, as one might build a cottage and make oneself at home in it. This world is not promised to us as Paradise. Rather, it is a place of conflicts, challenges, and crises. But the abysmal depths of Gethsemane are illuminated, indeed made possible, by the moment of rapture on the heights of Tabor. Jesus' disciples may feel anxiety in the overshadowing cloud from heaven, but it is still important for them to listen to Jesus, whom God loves and calls "my chosen Son." This is the message that incorporates everything Jesus wanted to communicate to us. We should see ourselves as children of light, as sons and daughters of the sun, as brothers and sisters in God's eyes. That is the height at which we should place and value human beings. Such an attitude has the power to change the world.

8. *God for Us*

If God is for us, who can be against us? He who did not spare his own Son but handed him over for us all, how will he not also give us everything else along with him? Who will bring a charge against God's chosen ones? It is God who acquits us. Who will condemn? It is Christ [Jesus] who died, rather, was raised, who also is at the right hand of God, who indeed intercedes for us (Rm 8:31b-34).

Sometimes people write letters that contain their whole being, their whole life. Even if we had nothing from the apostle Paul except his letter to the community at Rome, we could say with confidence that we know this man from Tarsus in his deepest self. That is how fully he expresses himself in this one letter.

It is a strange fact that apparently only people who themselves have endured a great deal of suffering are able to tell essential truth to other people. Paul suffered profoundly over a question that reappears in every religion and in every human life. The problem is, what is the relationship between justice and love, the external order and that of the heart? How can we relate law and mercy? Paul was almost shattered by this question, but in his collapse he found access to the mystery of Jesus' death and resurrection. It is typical of people like Paul that they do not avoid suffering. They are not in search of shortcuts; they want clarity, and if they are presented with an essential problem, they bite down on it and will not let go of the question, come hell or high water, until they find an answer that is true.

Other people might have found their own answers to the question of law and mercy; they would not have considered it so essential, so important, so fundamental. Others would have found a way to live with it—but not the man Paul from the little city of Tarsus in Asia Minor. At that time there was a relatively small group of people in Israel, only about ten thousand in all, who were called the "Select," the "Perushim"—we would say, the "Pharisees." They were a kind of lay order. Paul joined them with the flaming enthusiasm of unqualified idealism, because this group believed, literally, that the whole truth of life and the universe was contained in the 663 laws of Israel, if people would just live them. If just once there could be a Sabbath that was kept purely and rightly in Israel, the Messiah and his reign would appear on earth immediately. And what was there to prevent a person of good will from keeping the 663 laws of the ancestors and the 2,000 or so oral interpretations of the rabbis and scribes?

God knows, Paul was not short on good will, and yet he suffered an almost fatal defeat when he tried to keep the law. But why? Paul had to experience something that only confronts us when we really intend and desire to do what is right. We just want to live *rightly,* as perfectly and completely as possible. But then there rise up in the human soul all those desires, longings, thoughts, and feelings that are not perfect, but just beginning to grow, that are not yet ripe, but just seeking a way to unfold, that cannot make any claim as yet to be right, but are still searching, still developing. We have to fight these feelings, suppress them, get rid of them; we have to begin to hate ourselves because of them, and to be afraid of ourselves because of them. In spite of all our good will and all our proper striving, our souls are torn to pieces. The thoughts we banish in the daytime visit us at night; the feelings we deliberately suppress ingratiate themselves against our will. No matter

how we try to avoid ourselves, we cannot do it, and that is what brought
Paul to despair. Two chapters before the text of today's reading, he
shouts out what he felt before he encountered Christ: "I do not do the
good I want, but I do the evil I do not want. . . . Who will deliver me
from this mortal body?" (Rm 7:19, 24).

We might think that Paul should have been wiser or, as we say,
smarter. Nobody must or should take the law so seriously. We have to
be ready to make exceptions, change our spots a little, or else we just
have to tell ourselves that maybe it is really not necessary to be so strict
about keeping the law.

Paul hated that kind of nonsense and wouldn't give it the time of
day, thank God, for his fidelity to the absolute was his salvation. Thank
God, too, that Paul was not satisfied with being like most Pharisees.
They only *do* what is right, but they do not notice that they have ceased
to *be* genuine, right human beings. They have their morality, their laws,
their rules, their orders, and they keep them all. They never have to
accuse themselves of anything, and they cannot understand it when
people tell them that it is impossible to be good simply for the sake of
having a clear conscience; that it is impossible to protect oneself from
life and avoid everything connected with real existence, simply in order
to go through the world as someone who is pure, correct, and proper.
When matched with people like that, others such as Anna Karenina or
Effi Briest will always fall ill or end in despair. But the Mr. Karenins
will not change. They will not understand the weakness of their fellow
human beings, their excesses, their lack of good will, their insecurity
and despair, because they know what is right: 663 laws and 2,000
interpretations. Why don't people just follow them?

Thank God, Paul could not do it. He tried one more time. There was
a little group of people in Israel who believed in a man who evidently
had been crucified just in time. He was said to have come forward with
a strange kind of teaching: that human need and hunger gave people
the right to gather grain and eat it, even on the Sabbath!—that instead
of stoning an adulterous woman one could let her go because the one
who accused her was no better than she—that God desires mercy and
not sacrifice—and so on. Paul hated those people. He wanted to kill
them, just as their founder had been killed. His own heart was crying
out for pardon and mercy, but Paul did not want pardon or mercy; he
wanted no unmanly weakness and no lazy compromises. He wanted
the law, the whole law! So he became an informer, an inquisitor, a

persecutor, and a murderer, until he collapsed near Damascus and found himself in a fit of dizziness or enlightenment, hearing a voice from heaven that said: "Saul, why are you persecuting me?" Then, for the first time, Paul could not, would not, and dared not avoid a different law of life, one that in the future he never tired of proclaiming.

He was still convinced that the whole law of God written in the Old Testament was right, word for word, and that it had its place, its truth, and its justification. But when people ask why they are alive, what the purpose of their life could be, and then soothe their anxiety by clinging to the commandments, they become inhuman, stiff, unsympathetic, and vicious. At the beginning of his journey, Paul did not know that, but now he understood that God is for us, not against us. We do not need to appease God with our decency and perfection, as if God were one of our human judges or inquisitors. God wants us to live as we were made to live. We have no need to justify our existence by spotlessness, respectability, and decency. No one can accuse another, if God is on our side, and God *is* on our side. God does not grow in our hearts because of righteousness, but because of love. God's love has no limits. Paul's experience was that God gives us everything, especially our being alive, our existence, even if it involves a lot of twists, doubts, risks, hazards, searching, and seeking—our whole life. But this whole life of ours can be, should be, is free to be, in God's sight.

Now Paul stands up and asks, who can bring a charge against us, the chosen of God? That is how we should think about our relationship to God: Each individual one of us is not something special because we are faithful in keeping the law, but each of us is God's chosen one, someone pardoned for life. It is not we who justify ourselves; instead, God grows in our hearts, and that makes everything right. Paul is still talking like a lawyer when he asks, "Who will bring a charge against us, when Christ intercedes for us at the right hand of God?" This is still courtroom language, but Paul only uses it to be done with it once and for all.

We are children of light, Paul tells us, children of God, just as Jesus said. In our Father's house there are no orders, compulsion, oppression, terror, commandments, obedience, demands; instead there is love, acceptance, mercy, mutual support, and assistance, maturing in an atmosphere of warm affection. That is how life begins.

That is how Paul envisioned Christ's Church. It was not to be a place where one would say to another, "Tell how you have kept all the right laws just as you should, or do we first have to train you, set you straight, beat you up, or execute you?" The Church should be a place where the first question is: What kind of a being did God make you to be? What is your calling? What word called you into being, a word that can only be uttered in your living? Let me hear it. No matter how hesitantly, how anxiously, how tentatively you do it—say your word, find your song, discover your essential being. Then there will never again be anyone who is against you. For only love is eternal, more enduring than faith and hope. Only in love can the reign of God grow, and with it our humanity.

Third Sunday of Lent

9. God's Chosen

Moses was tending the flock of his father-in-law Jethro, the priest of Midian. Leading the flock across the desert, he came to Horeb, the mountain of God. There an angel of the Lord appeared to him in fire flaming out of a bush. As he looked on, he was surprised to see that the bush, though on fire, was not consumed. So Moses decided, "I must go over to look at this remarkable sight, and see why the bush is not burned." When the Lord saw him coming over to look at it more closely, God called out to him from the bush, "Moses! Moses!" He answered, "Here I am." God said, "Come no nearer! Remove the sandals from your feet, for the place where you stand is holy ground. I am the God of your father," he continued, "the God of Abraham, the God of Isaac, the God of Jacob." Moses hid his face, for he was afraid to look at God. But the Lord said, "I have witnessed the affliction of my people in Egypt and have heard their cry of complaint against their slave drivers, so I know well what they are suffering. Therefore I have come down to rescue them from the hands of the Egyptians and lead them out of that land into a good and spacious land, a land flowing with milk and honey, the country

*of the Canaanites, Hittites, Amorites, Perizzites, Hivites and
Jebusites. So indeed, the cry of the Israelites has reached me, and
I have truly noted that the Egyptians are oppressing them. Come,
now! I will send you to Pharaoh to lead my people, the Israelites,
out of Egypt." ... "But," said Moses to God, "when I go to the
Israelites and say to them, 'The God of your fathers has sent me
to you,' if they ask me, 'What is his name?' what am I to tell
them?" God replied, "I am who am." Then he added, "This is
what you shall tell the Israelites:* I AM *sent me to you." ... "But,"
objected Moses, "suppose they will not believe me, nor listen to
my plea? For they may say, 'The Lord did not appear to you.'"
The Lord therefore asked him, "What is that in your hand?" "A
staff," he answered. The Lord then said, "Throw it on the
ground." When he threw it on the ground it was changed into a
serpent, and Moses shied away from it. "Now, put out your
hand," the Lord said to him, "and take hold of its tail." So he
put out his hand and laid hold of it, and it became a staff in his
hand. "This will take place so that they may believe," he continued, "that the Lord, the God of their fathers, the God of Abraham,
the God of Isaac, the God of Jacob, did appear to you." ...
Moses, however, said to the Lord, "If you please, Lord, I have
never been eloquent, neither in the past, nor recently, nor now
that you have spoken to your servant; but I am slow of speech
and tongue." The Lord said to him, "Who gives one person
speech and makes another deaf and dumb? Or who gives sight
to one and makes another blind? Is it not I, the Lord? Go, then!
It is I who will assist you in speaking and will teach you what
you are to say" (Ex 3:1-10a, 13-14; 4:1-5, 10-12).*

Everything we know about Moses is wrapped in a cloak of saga and
legend, and yet his personality reaches out beyond the grave and across
more than three and a half millennia; it is as close to us as if we were
his contemporaries. This man's life really begins with a cry of rebellion
when, on reaching manhood, he had to witness the brutal murder of an
Israelite at the Egyptian court. The rage that gripped Moses was so
hot-blooded and uncontrolled that he became the murderer's murderer.
What he felt was genuine; it seized him like a divine force, a passion
of the heart for justice and for the freedom of every human being under
heaven. But it looked as if Moses' life was over before it began. For

fear of being hunted down and punished, he fled into the desert. There he married the daughter of a Midianite priest, who must have been very beautiful, because her name was Zipporah, "little bird." But Moses' heart was sad when he thought of the Hebrew people.

When can we say that God talks to a human being? Do human longing, human suffering, and the power of the human heart, when they are inflamed to the uttermost, project themselves into what we call God, so that we can give it the name of absolute duty, absolute greatness? Or should we say instead that we humans would not for a moment dare to fulfil the truth that is in us if we did not feel that we had been delegated and given authority by an Other who addresses us in this absolute fashion? According to the Bible, this is the only way we can understand the life of Moses. This person, who towers above his own time and his people even until today, shows himself in this story to be a man of such timidity and self-doubt that nothing would have happened without the truly fearful, scarcely bearable command of the Almighty: "And now, go!"

It all begins with a great vision that could well symbolize Moses' whole life, the vision of a bramble bush that burns but is not consumed. There is another passage in the Bible that can indicate what this means. Much later, when the people of Israel wanted to choose a king for themselves, someone who would lead and protect them, a man in Sichem named Abimelech made up his mind to be king. Then an early prophet went up on Mount Gerizim and sang a jeering song about how, once upon a time, the trees and bushes wanted to choose a king for themselves, and all the respectable plants refused to give up producing their sweetness and beauty to rule over the trees; only the bramble was willing to be king. This fable was supposed to show that, all in all, it is only the useless types who are most interested in power. Could it be the same way with Moses: that at the very moment when he wants to become the leader of the people, with God to back him up, he will show himself to be nothing but arrogant and proud and no better than a bramble bush? In the prophet's song, fire comes out of the bramble and devours the trees. Could it not be that Moses is taking his people by the hand only to lead them astray, relying on the freedom and independence of human beings? This suspicion underlies everything the Bible will later have to say about Israel's journey through the desert. Doubt dogs their every step, and most of all, it torments Moses. In the end, is it not possible that he has followed a demon, a delusion of his own heart, and wasn't everything he attempted doomed to failure? When we follow the voice of our own heart, where can we place our trust?

The vision of the burning bush is the mystery of the whole life of this great man at the beginning of Israel's religion. We human beings may be nothing, brambles in the desert, no good for anything except to be gnawed by wandering sheep and goats, but otherwise useless and of no value. If God wants to take possession of something like that, it will be with us as when fire takes hold of a bramble and reduces it to ashes. The miracle that Moses believes, and that shapes the whole religion of the Bible, is that God takes possession of this worthlessness that we are in such a way that God appears in us. God does not make us different, does not change our form, doesn't want us to be better than we are. Just as we are, we can bear the divine flame and pass it on. All that matters in our whole life is to sense what kind of fire it is that can take hold of us, and what passion is deep enough to express itself and to say that it can also take hold of the others who are with us, can snatch them up in freedom to cross over the deep gulf of the Red Sea.

As far as Moses' experience of himself is concerned, everything speaks against such a thing happening. It is not that, at this moment, he doubts the content of what he has to say: after all, it is truth itself, completely right and believable. The obstacle is his own self, as he knows it to be, and not just this minute, but yesterday and the day before, and always. The crucial objection is "brokenness," and Moses' stumbling speech expresses the way he feels himself to be.

When Moses says, "But, Lord . . . " he means: Everything you are saying ought to be and must be said, but not by me, because I am only Moses. And you will only be hurting your own cause if you choose me as your messenger. Look at the evidence. I am no speaker. Slow of speech and slow of tongue, that's me.

In all our lives there is no worse form of despair than to know what life could be like and what is necessary to make it so, but to see that the essential obstacle is everything we know about ourselves. The same man who struck down the Egyptian has such fiery zeal for freedom that it is eating him up, quite literally, but he is unable to shape words and speak slowly and produce patient explanations. Like all great visionaries, he wants God now, immediately, urgently, and as close as possible. It comes out of him like a cataract of unformed, illiterate speech. What can we do when we feel that we ourselves are obstacles to the truth and in such a terrible way? At this point, God tries an experiment with this man Moses.

"What is that in your hand?" God asks him. It could be a question for any of us in our self-doubt. We can feel comfortable in answering, "A staff. Something reliable that you can hold on to."

But there is nothing we can hold on to or rely upon when we are being pummeled by fear. "Throw it away!"

It is not the staff, but our whole life that we can release from our hands and simply let fall. Then we no longer have need of orders, and in some sense we have no need to be anxious any longer, except that we suddenly begin to be much more afraid of ourselves. First there is the fear that no one will believe us and we will not be able to explain the truth to anyone. But fear of other people very soon becomes fear of what is inside us, and a life of fear turns into a life of endless flight. There is nothing to do except to listen again to what God says in this test of our existence as illustrated in this example. "Put out your hand and take hold of its tail!"

This courage to act makes us and our life something solid and strong again, but not because we are that way ourselves. It is not a question of gritting our teeth and exhibiting some heroic self-confidence, but of having a little confidence in ourselves because we trust in God. The same is true of our whole body and soul. We can put our hands in our pockets because we are afraid. Then we are so stiff with fear that we can do nothing at all, and the result will be that people will start to run away from us because we are rotting. People who are crushed by fear cannot bear the presence of anyone else. There is no other remedy for fear than to do what we fear most: to be ourselves and to bring out what we have, what we hold in our hands.

Then comes what may be the most astonishing verse in the whole Bible, certainly one subject to misunderstanding, but with the same power to heal as a poison taken in medicinal quantities, if we can really accept it when God asks, "Who gives one person speech and makes another deaf and dumb? Or who gives sight to one and makes another blind?"

Ultimately, it seems that we should no longer see our faults and failings as accusations against God, but as something that we have received from God. Two things stand in contrast: Moses' "I," with its negative experiences, and God's "I," who desires everything that we are and are not. In any case, it is *enough* for God, in God's hands.

And so, finally, God says again, "Then go!"

It is a command, but grammatically it is in the future tense, and we can translate it better by saying: "And now you may go, now you can go, and therefore you will do what you most long to do and most passionately feel you should do: By obeying me, you will become fully and completely what you are."

There is a long bridge of three biblical books from here to the point, in the last chapter of Deuteronomy, when Moses stands on Mount Nebo and sees all Israel before him, from Dan to Beersheba and Jericho in its palm-ringed oasis. But because of his doubt, he will not enter the promised land. Nevertheless, this text assures us, there was never again a prophet in Israel like Moses, whose eyes were clear even in old age, and whose hands were strong, who did such signs and wonders before God and all the people. No one knows where he lies buried. Here Judaism makes a very fine distinction. Our Bible translations say, "Then Moses . . . died as the Lord had said," but literally it says, "Then Moses . . . died at the mouth of the Lord." So many Jews thought, and think, that Moses' death carried him to the mouth of the Lord, because he, a man with a broken mouth, had become the one who proclaimed the word of God. Then dying would mean nothing but that, at the moment of death, God's mouth kisses the soul away. No prophet in Israel was so human, to the very edge of despair, and for that very reason able to speak of God, and all Israel will never be anything other than what it became through Moses: constantly seeking and doubting and suffering under the burden of being called, and always too weak to have God on its lips, but still a bramble bush that never burns away.

10. Are Only Good People Lucky?

At that time some people who were present there told him about the Galileans whose blood Pilate had mingled with the blood of their sacrifices. He said to them in reply, "Do you think that because these Galileans suffered in this way they were greater sinners than all other Galileans? By no means! But I tell you, if you do not repent, you will all perish as they did! Or those eighteen people who were killed when the tower at Siloam fell on them—do you think they were more guilty than everyone else who lived in Jerusalem? By no means! But I tell you, if you do not repent, you will all perish as they did!" (Lk 13:1-5).

This is one of the very few gospel texts in the New Testament that address what is probably the most frightening question involved in the relationship of human beings to God: that of the injustice done to people by other people and by natural disasters. In many other places, Christ speaks of the confidence we may and should have in God's guidance, in spite of all our fears and lamentations. But here people are coming to him, horrified by what has happened and further agitated by their own judgment against God, which forces Christ to take a position unlike any other he expresses elsewhere.

We should be aware of the unhappy situation of the people who are coming to Christ. How can such a thing happen? People are standing at the altar, worshiping in God's presence, when godless heathens treacherously fall upon them and turn the people themselves into hideous sacrificial offerings. How can the God in whom we believe, the God we worship, permit such things?

This question is so terrible that Israel had spent centuries in search of a satisfactory answer. "God is just," said the theologians, the priests, and scribes. God must have reasons for allowing such things to happen. There is no error in the Eternal One, so when it seems that injustice has overtaken some people, that is only surface appearance. The All-Knowing One certainly knows the hidden faults in human hearts and punishes them, taking revenge on the secret guilt of those who are apparently innocent. This is a theology that lets God off the hook. But Christ says that it is inhuman; it balances accounts between God and human beings at the expense of mercy, and in the end what happens is that the unlucky have moral judgment added to whatever else they have suffered. The Lord vetoes that idea. He says we simply cannot think that way. To repeat, this is one of the very few places in the New Testament where Christ sees himself compelled by his own goodness to reveal the face of God and to distinguish the image of his Father from that of human beings.

He gives a second example. In Siloam, a tower has fallen and killed a group of people. The accident has created a sensation, and again there is an outraged cry. How can God permit such a thing? The explanation given is the same: There must be reasons known only to God's wisdom, probably the hidden wrongs committed by these people. Christ says first of all that it is impossible to make distinctions between the righteous and the unrighteous, the guilty and the innocent, and we certainly cannot appeal to the difference between the fortunate and the unfortunate, those who fall victim and those who escape. It is not so simple. We cannot say that those who are luckier than others are thereby shown to be better persons. This hidden Calvinistic equation does not work out in real life. That is the primary point Christ wants to make. But what kind of image of God do we get as a result?

We are accustomed to seek and find God in the processes of nature. We stand in awe before the works of God's creative power. They make our existence possible, and they give us space and a short period of time in which to live. Every detail, even the tiniest, is orderly, and the wisdom hidden in every atom is far too great for our imagining. But this nature takes no particular account of us humans. One tiny blood clot, one little embolism is enough to extinguish forever the fire of the spirit in the brain of a genius; all it takes is a little obstacle in a cardiac artery, and a heart full of love becomes cold and dead. In seconds, the laws of nature determine life or death; in its course we ourselves are children of coincidence, the offspring of impenetrable night.

We admire the laws of nature that make our lives possible, but both Christianity and Judaism were ill advised to make us believe that we could expect the laws of nature to take particular account of human questions, that we could find in them some kind of moral order measuring right and wrong. Because this has been taught for such a long time in the name of religion, in the last two centuries atheism has fed on people's despair in face of a natural order that has nothing to do with morality. The great Georg Büchner describes the poet Lenz, who sought advice from the Protestant pastor Oberlin in Steintal. Oberlin was a friend of Goethe, a genius of humanity. If there was any person of that era in whom humanity and piety were one, whose life was devoted to establishing kindergartens, building hospitals, and composing love songs to God, it was Pastor Oberlin. Lenz, terrified by the thoughts in his own heart and driven to the brink of insanity, turned to him, hoping to find comfort in the words of this man who was almost a saint. The horror that Büchner describes is that he did not find it. A baby was dying there in Steintal. Lenz stood by it and prayed over it the same words that Christ spoke to the daughter of Jairus. He returned to Oberlin faint and confused. "If I were that powerful," he stammered—"If I were, I would save them all. But God doesn't, won't, can't, that's the truth. If God wanted to change things, just in one tiny detail, maybe for the sake of the most precious person alive, the whole arch of the firmament would crash down in that instant. It has been formed in millions of years, over the lifetimes of millions, and it cannot feel concern for a single individual. This is nature, majestically great and, for our human understanding, horrible and often incomprehensible."

Therefore in the figure of Christ we have another, parallel, almost contradictory way of seeing and recognizing God that, at the same time, is just as true, just as absolute, just as genuine. We human beings can find a human way to approach God only in the company of another human being. That is the truth of Christianity; its single and most beautiful truth, if you like. If we carry an image of God in our hearts that surpasses that of the majestic God of creation, a human image of God, we can do so because we encounter other people who live their lives trusting in God. Whenever one of us is so marked by a person we love that our very being changes to be more like that person, we are very close to the God of our hearts. In the universe, we are a tiny fleck of mold on a pinpoint planet on the edge of the Milky Way. Only love can discover another human being, so very tiny, as infinitely great and important for all eternity. Only in love do we humans have a value that lasts forever, and only love can believe in our immortality. That we are called to this is something we can only learn in the presence of another human being who loves us very much, and whom we love in return. We can reach heaven only in pairs. That is just what Christ, in his goodness and understanding, wants to teach us. Nature may be grim, but we can take one another by the hand and go on loving one another all the more. It may be that we cannot protect ourselves or rescue one another from the dangers of life outside, but we can stand together inside, and that will never end, in time or eternity. For that very reason the misfortune that happens to people should be no argument for separation, and it cannot promote any division between right and wrong. There is only one realm of humanity and goodness. The fact that no one can judge another is among the most precious things the

Lord wanted to teach us. The only thing we can judge is the lack of good will in our own hearts. As this Gospel teaches us, the time we have left for learning kindness with and for one another is not unlimited.

11. What Price God?

Since the Passover of the Jews was near, Jesus went up to Jerusalem. He found in the temple area those who sold oxen, sheep, and doves, as well as the money-changers seated there. He made a whip out of cords and drove them all out of the temple area, with the sheep and oxen, and spilled the coins of the money-changers and overturned their tables, and to those who sold doves he said, "Take these out of here, and stop making my Father's house a marketplace." His disciples recalled the words of scripture, "Zeal for your house will consume me." At this the Jews answered and said to him, "What sign can you show us for doing this?" Jesus answered and said to them, "Destroy this temple and in three days I will raise it up." The Jews said, "This temple has been under construction for forty-six years, and you will raise it up in three days?" But he was speaking about the temple of his body. Therefore, when he was raised from the dead, his disciples remembered that he had said this, and they came to believe the scripture and the word Jesus had spoken.

While he was in Jerusalem for the feast of Passover, many began to believe in his name when they saw the signs he was doing. But Jesus would not trust himself to them because he knew them all, and did not need anyone to testify about human nature. He himself understood it well (Jn 2:13-25).

The first three Gospels place it at the end, and the fourth Gospel at the beginning of Jesus' public activity; but in fact the cleansing of the Jerusalem Temple expresses the meaning of Jesus' whole life.

There are people who fall into conflict with official religion because they find its essential content to be empty and meaningless. Philosophers, artists, scholars in every century have distanced themselves, either privately or publicly, from the religious systems of their times. There are other people whose relationship to the religious establishment is tense because they take religion more seriously than even its official representatives want it to be. The prophets of every age have been people like that. But even this type can be subdivided.

It is possible to take religion seriously in such a way that we cling to it in terror, like a drowning person, and with the best will in the world ask religion to preserve us, strengthen us, and maintain an impenetrable armor for us against fear. In Jesus' time, this kind of protest was concentrated in the desert monastics at Qumran. They cursed the Temple at Jerusalem, called it a foreign, blasphemous institution, and did not want to soil their hands with the impious sacrifices of the priesthood installed by the Pharisees.

But there is also a different and opposite way of taking religion seriously, to the point that it becomes bitter and painful: by demanding of it so much freedom from fear, so much humanity, and so much daring that it terrifies those who want to control it. This latter form is embodied in the person of Jesus of Nazareth. The cleansing of the Temple was not a unique moment of rebellion, a passing symbol that was only accidentally related to the rest of his life; instead, it expressed all that he really wanted. It must have started right away, at the beginning of his public activity, when on a Sabbath day in the synagogue at Capernaum he defied the Pharisees and scribes by placing a cripple in the middle of the gathering. "Tell me," he said, as excited and angry as in that later moment when he cleansed the Temple, "is it permitted to do good on the Sabbath, or to do evil?" That is, must one do evil by keeping one's hands clean, maintaining the proper order prescribed by the Sabbath commandment, or should one instead, out of sheer necessity, tread underfoot a written commandment of God so important that to violate it is death, rather than trample violently and brutally on the life of another human being? This crippled man standing there appeared in Jesus' eyes as someone beaten down and pressed to earth by the burden of an authoritarian order of obedience to the law. What would God have done in this moment? The Sabbath order was justified by the argument that God had also rested on the seventh day and found that the creation was very good. But a suffering human being is a contradiction of God's Sabbath rest, and when someone is suffering it is impossible for the Sabbath to be very good. If God saw this twisted body, how could or would God resist perfecting the work once begun? But God can only do that through our humanity. *That* is what it means to purify and reform and humanize God's Sabbath order.

Thus from Jesus' first word and action the lines were drawn, and so it continued to this scene in Jerusalem. Here he is at the head of the group of people who followed him because they were desperate enough to know what grace is and hopeless enough to believe in nothing but God, and who prayed as Jesus taught them: Father, may your reign come. Here, in the place where the word of God is proclaimed in Jerusalem, Jesus demands mercy and humanity of those who are in charge: high priests, scribes, Pharisees. Jesus cannot have been ignorant of the fact that underneath, these things were connected. What he did again and again in Galilee, in the villages around the Lake of Gennesaret, we describe (in theological pablum-language) as "forgiving sins." This expression is so dusty and so shopworn, it has been so bejeweled and shrouded in mystery, that no one gets anything out of it any more. If instead of saying "he forgave their sins," we were to say "he fought against every kind of alienation, oppression, anxious dependency, and internalized violence," we would be calling things by their right names. For Jesus saw that in the name of God the ordinary country people were being repeatedly bound in the chains of an ethic of obedience that suffocated them and forbade them to live, and that ultimately made God a tyrant to be feared and avoided, instead of someone to be trusted, someone to whom one could open oneself. This kind of religion maligns God, who is fatherly and motherly to human beings and wants us to be sisters and brothers who know how to live together.

This God-language, which on the one hand is a tyranny, is, from another point of view, a matter of cause and effect, purpose and goal, a well-thought-out, fully calculated system of power and the acquisition of wealth. It was this barbaric exterior of organized religion that Jesus encountered in the Temple in Jerusalem, where the head of the whole affair is located and where all the threads are drawn together, where the decision makers have their seats and whence every regulation proceeds. We usually hear that Jesus talks lovingly to others in a language that comes from and speaks to the heart. He could be infinitely kind and understanding, but at this moment he is seized by rage, expressed in the prophetic phrase, "zeal for God." What he does is unmistakable. There is no more talk. He does what we would scarcely think possible, if we did not know this Gospel. He makes a whip and strikes out against the people who quite possibly were not responsible—money-changers who exchanged Gentile coins for the Jewish shekel that, for ritual reasons, was the only money acceptable in the Temple, and those who sold sacrificial animals for the money thus exchanged, the sacrifices people had to bring to earn God's favor. Jesus is so enraged at this haggling in the holy place that he sweeps out whatever he can eject, because it has nothing to do with God.

And now the contrast must be quite clear, because from Jesus' time to this, the question has been: What does the way Jesus wanted to live with God tell us about God? We think that we in the Church have every right to appeal to the man of Nazareth: We bear his name, and we are bound to his existence, through baptism, for life and death. We gather around the Church's altar to say that he is like food and drink for us. But do we understand and live Jesus the way he wanted, as deeply, as passionately, as humanely? What does the Church we live in have to do with the prophet of Nazareth who commanded us to choose between God and money, between the Father in heaven and mammon, the anti-god? One might suppose that it is unavoidable that money must play a certain role within an institutional religion, although always in the service of the holy and for charitable reasons, for necessary and justified expenses: building funds, personal gifts, repairs. No Church that wishes to appear as a well-organized body of Christ, a perfect society, as it has been called since the sixteenth century, will be able to do without money—even the organ and the heat and the windows have to be paid for. All of that is true, as you must see if you can count to three. But Jesus did not want us to start counting, not even to three. He wanted people to think of God and look at human beings.

And so the question becomes: What is God worth to us? At what price can we afford not to externalize religion? In Jesus' time it was possible to personalize every problem. The Temple confines within which the haggling went on belonged to Annas, the high priest, father-in-law of the later high priest Caiaphas who opposed Jesus and obtained the death sentence against him. Somewhere or other there are always groups who profit from religion, and we ought to expose their alibis.

The same can be summarized in two points that pretend to furnish structural stability for religion but really undermine it.

First, the experience of personal encounter with God is transformed into an external doctrine, the very doctrine of legality and compulsion that Jesus found manifested in human hearts in the form of possession and sickness, and that he tried to banish. Let us put it to the test: How does Christianity present itself? If we are honest, we cannot help admitting that at least since the fourth century the Church has existed almost exclusively as a teaching institution, directed by particular classes who interpret the way one must believe in Christ, that is, what formulas one must repeat in order to demonstrate that one believes in Christ. Anyone who does not know this language word for word does not count as a member of the Church and is to be expelled as an unbeliever. The maintenance of this system requires a lot of money for years of education, for the establishment of massive libraries, for building up a gigantic, pyramidal system of power distribution. Such a system is maintained by pretending to ordinary people that their experiences and feelings are of no value before God unless they are validated by the experts' language game. These experts know when one is a believer and on the right track, and as long as that is not the case, nothing we do is valid in relation to God or Jesus Christ.

What would Jesus do if he returned to this world, two thousand years later? What kind of whips would he have to wield to hit us? It takes a lot of power to keep this system operating. It takes access to the educational monopoly, it takes collaboration with the power of the state, it takes the support of the public authorities. Ultimately the Church is, in turn, a support for the civil order, producing its metaphysical justification of public ethics and its time-conditioned customs of the dominant form of its common life. As it becomes more and more dependent on the civil order, it gets farther and farther from God. Shouldn't we be consumed by sorrow when we see that the most precious achievements of Christianity in the West are its magnificent cathedrals, so beautiful that, as museums, they are a lofty testimony to the architectural achievements, stylistic taste, courage to sacrifice, and wealth of past eras—and how much blood is sticking to all that gold and money! The Roman basilicas are clad in the gold of the Aztecs, a culture dishonored and throttled—in the service of God, of course, but which God? The Father of Jesus Christ? Surely not.

Second, one must concede that all this is not merely external. It is not only the institution, but we ourselves who apparently wish for nothing better and are content to let things go on as they are. We cooperate in being led by the hand, and we fit in where we are supposed to. We do not dare to point out the difference between the golden Gospel books that are opened on lofty stands so that the word of Jesus may be carefully and wisely interpreted before emperors and kings, lords and governors, and St. Francis, who sold his last Bible to help a beggar. If God only speaks in our hearts, the message comes cheap, but we are very rich. Jesus wanted us to know that.

When Meister Eckhart preached on this Gospel in the Middle Ages, he said that the Temple of Jerusalem that Jesus cleansed is our heart. It is all there—the fear and the response to it, the lust for power, the desire for wealth, the spirit of subservience, the addiction. But there is also the longing for freedom, the courage to live, the joy of humanity, and the power of love. The part of the Temple Jesus cleansed was the court of the Gentiles. It was his desire that there should no longer be a religion that was closed to any human being who could be said to understand nothing about God. Every human person, even a Gentile, can find God without sacrifice and ritual, because as a human being, as the Father's creation, everyone is in the hands of the Eternal. Whoever finds God lives Jesus Christ. Whoever refuses, even in the most pious formula of words, betrays him on that day to Golgotha and Gethsemane.

12. Three Questions

Now when Jesus learned that the Pharisees had heard that Jesus was making and baptizing more disciples than John (although Jesus himself was not baptizing, just his disciples), he left Judea and returned to Galilee. He had to pass through Samaria. So he came to a town of Samaria called Sychar, near the plot of land that Jacob had given to his son Joseph. Jacob's well was there. Jesus, tired from his journey, sat down there at the well. It was about noon.

A woman of Samaria came to draw water. Jesus said to her, "Give me a drink." His disciples had gone into the town to buy food. The Samaritan woman said to him, "How can you, a Jew,

ask me, a Samaritan woman, for a drink?" (For Jews use nothing
in common with Samaritans.) Jesus answered and said to her, "If
you knew the gift of God and who is saying to you, 'Give me a
drink,' you would have asked him and he would have given you
living water." [The woman] said to him, "Sir, you do not even
have a bucket and the cistern is deep; where then can you get
this living water? Are you greater than our father Jacob, who
gave us this cistern and drank from it himself with his children
and his flocks?" Jesus answered and said to her, "Everyone who
drinks this water will be thirsty again; but whoever drinks the
water I shall give will never thirst; the water I shall give will
become in him a spring of water welling up to eternal life." The
woman said to him, "Sir, give me this water, so that I may not be
thirsty or have to keep coming here to draw water."

Jesus said to her, "Go call your husband and come back."
The woman answered and said to him, "I do not have a husband." Jesus answered her, "You are right in saying, 'I do not
have a husband.' For you have had five husbands, and the one
you have now is not your husband. What you have said is true."

The woman said to him, "Sir, I can see that you are a prophet.
Our ancestors worshiped on this mountain; but you people say
that the place to worship is in Jerusalem." Jesus said to her,
"Believe me, woman, the hour is coming when you will worship
the Father neither on this mountain nor in Jerusalem. You people
worship what you do not understand; we worship what we
understand, because salvation is from the Jews. But the hour is
coming, and is now here, when true worshipers will worship the
Father in Spirit and truth; and indeed the Father seeks such
people to worship him. God is Spirit, and those who worship him
must worship in Spirit and truth." The woman said to him, "I
know that the Messiah is coming, the one called the Anointed;
when he comes, he will tell us everything." Jesus said to her, "I
am he, the one who is speaking with you." . . .

Many of the Samaritans of that town began to believe in him
because of the word of the woman who testified, "He told me
everything I have done." When the Samaritans came to him, they
invited him to stay with them; and he stayed there two days. Many
more began to believe in him because of his word, and they said
to the woman, "We no longer believe because of your word; for

*we have heard for ourselves, and we know that this is truly the
savior of the world" (Jn 4:1-26, 39-42).*

There are texts in the New Testament that lie like undiscovered gems
in the dust of time and only reveal themselves slowly to our understanding. Two thousand years after this conversation between Jesus and
the woman at Jacob's well we are, quite literally, just beginning to
discover all that it has to tell us.

It begins with Jesus' having turned his back on Judea, where they
were debating the question of who was winning more disciples, Jesus
or John the Baptist. Jesus seems to have been so disgusted by this
compiling of statistics on religious affiliation and competition for
followers that he turned away from Judea, the place where God had
been proclaimed for centuries, and literally went to a religious back-
of-beyond. Samaria was a nation at enmity with orthodox believers,
and there had been centuries of national, religious, and political hatred
between the religion of the synagogue and these semi-Jews, worse than
the Gentiles because they had excluded themselves from the circle of
orthodoxy. This was the remnant of the ancient northern kingdom,
revived in Samaria, and political intrigues, rivalry between kings, and
religious ideology had separated the one people of the revelation, just
as in the Christian West not many decades ago Protestants and Catholics in many areas could see themselves as enemies because of the creed
that really belonged to all of them.

This Gospel reading thus begins with the question of how it is
possible to speak plausibly about God under such conditions, in a very
different context of understanding and with completely different preconditions. It is the question that occupies us Christians even to the
present day. How can we, as fathers or mothers, tell our children
something about God that they can believe? We preach our own
religious convictions to a world that apparently has no such questions,
and how can we speak of our faith in God, as embodied in Jesus, in the
context of very different religious histories?

If we think about it, we will see that this dialogue at Jacob's well
could never occur if we were to take this first question—how to preach
our faith in God—as the first and central problem. No part of this
conversation could have happened if at least three taboos had not been
overcome at the outset by the simple use of something like an international language of communication. Everything starts when Jesus is

tired and thirsty in the noonday heat and sits down at the well, and a woman comes to draw water. A self-respecting Jew would have shown some character and simply endured his thirst. He would have forbidden himself this contact with a non-Jew, a Samaritan, in this humble form of a request for water. Even as a man, it was his duty not to descend to the level of asking a woman to help him. The bonds of religion would require him bravely to deny his own need. It would not have been possible for this conversation that changed everything in the life of the woman of Sychar to have taken place, or even begun, if Jesus had not had the courage to overcome the taboos of nationality and religion and the moral barrier between man and woman in patriarchal society.

What is at stake here must be literally translated to the twentieth century, where national barriers are still erected against our humanity so that national interests, for example, still prevent us from being aware of hunger and thirst as world problems. But it is our duty as human beings to remember that, by the very fact that we have bodies that depend on the cycle of energy and food, we are all one in these elemental experiences. Everyone in this world knows what weariness, hunger, and thirst are, and yet a boundary marker can show that we are light-years away from one another.

The darkness of religion can consist in helping only those who "belong" to us. I remember that years ago, in the last days before Christmas when we were taking up the Advent collection for world charity ("Adveniat"), there was another collection being taken up in the streets for refugees in Bangladesh, more than twelve million of whom had been expelled from Bengal. "You can't do that," I heard someone say. "You mustn't compete with us; we are collecting for Adveniat." But what are we taking up our collection for? To demonstrate our own power, the financial advantages of the strong? Or is it because we know that people who are sleeping on newspapers need our help, no matter what color they are, what language they speak, or what religion they belong to?

When will a man in our society, especially in our religion, dare to say to a woman, "Please give me a glass of water"? Even if the water were not symbolic, if he were dying of thirst and needed help not just from anybody, but from that very person, man or woman, we would already be in the realm of indecency, of the apparently forbidden, of things laden with taboos. How free do you have to be to be human?

Without this fundamental humanity, not one word of this dialogue could have been spoken. But then Jesus immediately anticipates the end of the whole matter and says: "If you knew who it is who is speaking with you!" What we need in life is never just *something,* but the encounter with a person, and we will never find rest on this earth until behind everything else we can perceive an absolute, a person who wants us to live. But how can we arrive at this insight?

When Jesus speaks the language of religion, it reveals itself right away as full of possible misunderstandings. There is the image of the water of life. For a moment the woman at Jacob's well interprets it in her own way. The only inheritance that remains from father Jacob in the Old Testament—the tribal ancestor of Israel, the man who dreamed of God and tried to make his way in the world, the man who loved and wooed Rachel—is his well, where he and his servants and his animals drank. It can happen to us all that way, that the heart of everything desirable remains at the level of human need. Bodily nourishment would be a tremendous thing for all those who are able to gain it only through strenuous effort or self-denial, and it would be practically a dream of paradise for them to think that they no longer needed any of the daily grind that goes with earning the barest minimum for existence. Yet that is not what makes us human. Even supposing we all lived the way some of us do at the end of the twentieth century in Germany—above the level of need or of anxiety about securing our physical existence, with running water in our houses and all the means at our disposal to make ourselves fairly comfortable, in wealth beyond the ancient Pharaohs' wildest dreams—would we have reached the end of our longing and striving? We would soon realize something that we here in Western Europe may know better than the people of the Third World: hunger, poverty, thirst, weariness, sorrow, loneliness, despair, and sickness can still visit us *within* much more poignantly than was ever the case with our external troubles. Ultimately we *have* everything, and still we do not know why we *are*. We only have to look in the refrigerator to know what we have to live on, but we do not know why. What is the purpose of our lives? There seems to be a world separating us from that knowledge.

That is the second question Jesus poses to this woman at Jacob's well: What is the real source of her life? Jesus tells her bluntly, "You have had five husbands, and the one you have now is not your husband." We human beings look for others to cling to. Only in their eyes can we see ourselves as somehow beautiful, only in their words will we feel ourselves somehow justified, and only at their side will we find something like security and peace. Where are such people to be found? This woman has looked and looked, more than most, and she has been repeatedly disappointed and started her search all over again. It can happen that we have bad luck in our search for happiness, and we go around and around in circles without knowing how to reach our goal.

Nowadays I often hear it said that there is a vast difference between a religion like Christianity and purely human striving for self-fulfil-ment, and that the two are incompatible. This reading from John 4 may show us that we will not find God in any other way than by understand-ing at least the reasons why we are unhappy. At this point Jesus helps the woman to understand what she is looking for, what she wants, and what it is that keeps throwing her back into disappointments and blind alleys. Only at this point, when the woman's life is sorted out, does their conversation turn to religion. Here the contrast is renewed: You Jews worship in Jerusalem, we Samaritans on Gerizim, and which of the religions our ancestors taught us is correct, which is true? Jesus evokes a shocking breath from the dawn of history when he addresses the life of this woman. It is not a question of fixing belief through its origins and traditions. What God wants are people who turn to God out of their own inner truth and spirit, out of a solid conviction. Everything the woman has learned in this dialogue enters into her own truth and reality.

Then comes the question: How can such a conviction in spirit and truth be articulated and expressed? Could it not be that we know everything and yet do not know how to live, here and now? In our Church we so often hear it said that we should not be impatient. We cannot expect changes *immediately,* and everything comes to those who wait. We wait and wait until the twelfth of never. So this woman, in her faith and confusion, says, "I know that the Messiah is coming, and will explain everything to us. But when?" There is only *one* way to live as a Christian: "Who, if not I, and when, if not now?"—and no delay is permitted. Then we will see, in the person of Jesus of Nazareth, that the barriers between heaven and earth are opened and there is no longer any opposition between God and human beings or between the language of religion and that of human self-fulfillment, and that there is no longer any basis for barriers between human beings here on earth.

Even the people in Sychar will say, later on, "We no longer believe because of what you said, woman, for we have heard it ourselves." If we could understand this Gospel as a dialogue in stages, a difficult journey to knowledge, we would be approaching the world religion of brother- and sisterhood that we as *one* humanity need. Christianity is still separated into various confessions, and religions are still divided according to their different beliefs, but could it not be possible that we need all of them and that each could contribute its experiences instead of its doctrines? Then this Gospel would tell us to learn from the Buddhists who spend their whole lives in seeking to experience what it means to go on in an endless cycle, driven by the compulsions of thirst to seek the same well again and again. Life's thirst tortures us because it can never be satisfied. That experience is the heart of Buddhism.

A man and woman seek each other, and in doing so search for God. They do not fear their bodiliness and sensuality, but in their desire allow them to be ensouled until they arrive at eternity. This is the way of Hinduism in its myths, its poetry, its love lyrics, and the incomparable literature of all the forces of nature in and around human beings. The anticipation that our history will be fulfilled in the coming of the Messiah and that there will really be a reign of God among human beings is the legacy of Judaism and Islam.

We need all these religions; they do not contradict one another, and we need them to understand what we ourselves believe. They could all be part of the sanctuary of Christ, who said: "I am." This is the reality of someone entirely free, a person who is ready to take each of us by the hand so that we may become like God, a person alive in freedom, rooted in love, dependent as a creature, but called to infinity.

Fourth Sunday of Lent

13. The Price of Freedom

In their thirst for water, the people grumbled against Moses, saying, "Why did you ever make us leave Egypt? Was it just to have us die here of thirst with our children and our livestock?" So Moses cried out to the Lord, "What shall I do with this people? A little more and they will stone me!" The Lord answered Moses, "Go over there in front of the people, along with some of the elders of Israel, holding in your hand, as you go, the staff with which you struck the river. I will be standing there in front of you on the rock in Horeb. Strike the rock, and the water will flow from it for the people to drink." This Moses did, in the presence of the elders of Israel. The place was called Massah and Meribah, because the Israelites quarreled there and tested the Lord, saying, "Is the Lord in our midst or not?" (Ex 17:3-7).

These stories about Israel's exodus from Egypt are remarkable and strange. For generations, the people had lived in a land they would later, in retrospect, call "the fiery furnace" and "the house of slavery." They never would have gone to Egypt had they not been driven by hunger, but they bought their provisions at the price of living in a foreign country and without rights. Every day they had to earn their residence permit by bowing their backs under the lash of their drivers. They no longer had any hope that their toil would yield happiness for a future generation, for at Pharaoh's command their firstborn, and every male child, was to be destroyed.

In the midst of this grueling pain and endless suffering, God heard the cries of the people and gave them the command that comes to everyone who can no longer endure human slavery and fear: "Depart from this land again, and choose your freedom." Israel went, just as any of us enters into freedom when we are afraid—by night and fog, in flight, until at the shores of the Red Sea they saw no further path before them and heard the hoofbeats of the tyrant's chariot brigade close behind them: no way forward and no retreat. They would have despaired had not Moses, standing on the opposite shore, stretched out his staff over the water and said to the people: "Come, put your foot on what you think is an abyss; take a road you have never followed before; go straight ahead, even if you feel like blind people; for there is only this one way, and everything else is death. Choose life by forgetting your fear. Keep going straight ahead."

It was on the other shore that Israel began to learn to live all over again. The prophets would later say that it was this people's happiest time. There were no more provisions in reserve. There was no way to go on relying on human security, nothing to do, nothing to achieve as a basis for future security or a pattern on which to model that future. They lived, literally, from hand to mouth and day to day, and they did not know what it was that sustained them. They called it "what is it?"—the word is *manhu*. But they did not begin a single morning without being thankful for the gift of life, for being saved by some miracle, and they gathered pieces of something from the ground that tasted sweet as honey cakes in their mouths. It was a time of unfettered freedom, the broad places of the heart, the early dawn at the beginning of a new world.

But the day came when the price of freedom seemed too high, the effort and tedium of the road too great, every resting place only the beginning of a new exodus. The people rose up in a revolution of weariness, resignation, impatience, and exhaustion. They began to wonder if what Moses was doing was not just a terrible mistake, and if God was really in the midst of the people as their support and protector, or whether this was all madness and imagination. They began to talk about how nice it had been in Egypt, where they had an income and a livelihood. They had melons and cucumbers to eat there, leeks and lettuce; they were taken care of, and is a secure life not much better than a free life lived in uncertainty? They hated Moses and cursed him. But Moses had no answer except to say, Your God is on Mount Horeb. There is no enduring solution to your problems, no fairyland or paradise on earth. But we need know nothing more about God, except that God is here and gives us life *today.* In the words of the New Testament, take no thought for tomorrow; God is there as the one who is and will be. That is the only basis for your life.

Then Moses went up onto the highest peak of Mount Pisgah, called Nebo, and stood there and saw the whole land that was called "promised," from Dan to Beersheba, from north to south. He could not enter it himself, and perhaps that was as it should be, for they had scarcely entered it before they had to fight for every city and every place in that promised land. Almost as soon as it was gained, the kingdom melted like snow in the sun; Jerusalem, a walled city, was filled with blood. "If I forget you, Jerusalem, let my right arm wither," the pious prayed in their exile. The promised land was never promised; it was all a dream.

But we have learned from that dream that it is worthwhile to travel together, even to the end of the world, for wherever we go, God will be waiting for us. It will not be an earthly paradise, but it will be a constant presence that will be fulfilled in eternity. Here on earth, God already gives us the strength to strike water from the rock.

The present adult generation lays on its parents the guilt for World War II and the horrible massacre of the chosen people—more than fifty million dead between 1939 and 1945. "Where were you?" this generation asks its parents, who know many things that could serve as excuses and would make every accusation appear unjust. What will the coming generation say about us when it discovers that in a single year fifty million suffering people die of hunger while in the northern hemisphere our stomachs and our markets are full to bursting? If all this human ruin and suffering were happening 100 kilometers from us instead of 10,000, the police would be in our houses arresting us for failing to give aid. We have no international police, but do we therefore have a right to live like stone age people, with every hunting party sitting and smacking its lips around its capture and fighting off the neighboring horde? Then we go to the altar and celebrate a meal together, a meal to which every human being is invited? It is hard to bear the burden of guilt that belongs to our own time.

I am only a priest. When Moses saw that, even after all that had happened on the desert journey, the people were beginning to worship the golden calf, he took the tables of the law and smashed them on the rock. God's own finger had written on the stone: You shall not kill. And the stone let itself be inscribed. But where can we find words to write on human hearts? How does one rescue a new generation from suffocating because all their questions about meaning, emotions, and truth are only answered with platitudes about what one must do in order to earn money, to succeed, and to maintain one's own life? How do we prevent them from being strangled by pure meaninglessness and boredom?

We are standing face-to-face with an ultimate choice. Either we learn in freedom to put an end to what we call rationality and politics, namely the expansion of a boundless group-egoism expressed in national competition, or it will happen as it has always happened throughout history, when it is too late. Want will rise up with violence and dictatorship and force changes in a bloody and gruesome fashion, creating new forms of inhumanity.

I know that individuals are not much and that they are incapable of effective action. But that does not prevent those who are tired of listening to the discussion about whether we should devote .37% of our gross national product to development aid, or whether we should give .7%, as we spoke of doing a dozen years ago, from finding all this talk barbaric and mad. It seems obvious that we should be giving ten times that much. And we should be able to hope that there may be Church leaders and national officials who will say that we can only survive as a single humanity if our life is founded on sharing and no longer on possessing, on the feeling of universal solidarity and not on the private egoism of some kind of nation-state.

The sign of the one who sacrificed himself for humanity is true. We live from our self-giving to one another. As long as there are people in the *favelas* of São Paulo, in the slums of Madras, Bombay, and Calcutta who envy the rats because they can eat the garbage, people whose sustenance comes from the sewers and garbage dumps where all they gather is sickness and infection—as long as that is the case, we have no right to feel contented and settled in this world. We have the marvelous opportunity to strike water from the rock for one another on this short stretch of the journey; we have the chance to be *one* people gathered in the shelter of *one* God. In the end, God will never ask us about anything other than what we did for our sisters and our brothers. That is the only yardstick that will be applied. Today mercy may seem weak, but tomorrow it will be a power that conquers the world.

14. Dead and Alive

Then he said, "A man had two sons, and the younger son said to his father, 'Father, give me the share of your estate that should come to me.' So the father divided the property between them. After a few days, the younger son collected all his belongings and set off to a distant country where he squandered his inheritance on a life of dissipation. When he had freely spent everything, a severe famine struck that country, and he found himself in dire need. So he hired himself out to one of the local citizens who sent him to his farm to tend the swine. And he longed to eat his fill of the pods on which the swine fed, but nobody gave him any. Coming to his senses he thought, 'How many of my father's hired workers have more than enough food to eat, but here am I, dying from hunger. I shall get up and go to my father and I shall say to him, "Father, I have sinned against heaven and against you. I no longer deserve to be called your son; treat me as you would treat one of your hired workers." ' So he got up and went back to his father. While he was still a long way off, his father caught sight of him, and was filled with compassion. He ran to his son, embraced him and kissed him. His son said to him, 'Father, I have sinned against heaven and against you; I no longer deserve to be called your son.' But his father ordered his servants, 'Quickly bring the finest robe and put it on him; put a ring on his finger and sandals on his feet. Take the fattened calf and slaughter it. Then let us celebrate with a feast, because this son of mine was dead, and has come to life again; he was lost, and has been found.' Then the celebration began. Now the older son had been out in the field and, on his way back, as he neared the house, he heard the sound of music and dancing. He called one of the servants and asked what this might mean. The servant said to him, 'Your brother has returned and your father has slaughtered the fattened calf because he has him back safe and sound.' He became angry, and when he refused to enter the house, his father came out and pleaded with him. He said to his father in reply, 'Look, all these years I served you and not once did I disobey your orders; yet you never gave me even a young goat to feast on with my friends. But when your son returns who swallowed up your property with prostitutes, for him you slaughter the fattened calf.' He said to him, 'My son, you are here with me always; everything I have is yours. But now we must celebrate and rejoice, because your brother was dead and has come to life again; he was lost and has been found' " (Lk 15:11-32).

Jesus rarely expresses his own concerns as urgently and concisely as in this parable of the two sons. We have to have a clear picture of the scene, as Jesus is telling the story. People have been coming to Christ from throughout the whole region, people who could find neither faith nor hope in their lives: desperate people, people deprived of all rights, people generally regarded as worthless. They believe that the man from Nazareth can restore to them some dignity and a feeling for their true worth. With him, they think they can find a foothold, and that is just what Christ wants: that the lost and the strays be led back to God. "I did not come for those who are well," he said, "but for the sick." He teaches that God has more joy in the hundredth sheep, when it returns, than in the ninety-nine others who have no need of repentance. His whole desire was that people would think of God, whom he called his Father, only as kind, understanding, and open-hearted, a God who does not put up barriers or set boundaries. That in itself was a scandal to those who never neglected to worship God in the synagogue or in the Temple on the Sabbath, whose lips were constantly forming prayers, and whose hearts were filled by the words of the law. These people, the upright, the blameless, pushed themselves between Christ and the crowds of the lost. They had an interest in cutting the bond of understanding, because they were sure that God's love has conditions attached, conditions they knew and understood, and without which they became anxious.

Christ wants to establish a connection that would bridge these divisions of law and scorn, piety and misery, worship of God and hardness of heart. He wants to bring together all the people of Israel, to explain the feelings of one party to the other, and to awaken in every heart a willingness to approach the others. So he tells this parable of the two sons.

The figure of the father as he portrays him cannot be identified with God without qualification, and yet their features overlap, for the portrait of this active oriental gentleman is quite remarkable. It must have been difficult for him to hear his younger son pronounced dead while still alive. "The share of your estate that should come to me"— every word, in a certain sense, is insulting and mean, but this father does not choose to be insulted or demeaned. He accedes to his son's impetuous desire for freedom, knowing that there are no means of persuasion that are effective against the feeling of being tied down and dependent except generosity and open-heartedness and trust. But can a man have such virtues in this situation? Later we learn that at the moment the son leaves, his father regards him as dead. "My son was dead," he will say; that is how deeply he has felt his anxiety, bitterness, and fear. But he is understanding enough not to utter a syllable that would betray his feelings. He acts as if it all doesn't matter, and he hopes that his son will find what he is seeking: genuine freedom, or at least a freedom that is not blocked by his father's affection.

Now, in this son, the Lord paints the portrait of all the lost, all the strays in Israel. He portrays sin as the story of freedom betrayed. That is how it begins, says Christ: We think we can only be human and in full possession of ourselves when we leave our parents' house and the narrow ghetto of our obligations. Those seem to be the strong characters, the people who fight their way out into a different, distant, free life. The promise of unalloyed freedom is the seductive power that leads us into misery. Soon we discover that on this road we do not become rich and important, but only poor and diminished. The impetuous search for freedom turns to sheer hunger, utter misery, until finally we are glad to be enslaved and to fall to the level of pigs, or even below the pigs, just to maintain our existence. Our burning shame forces us to keep on the same course as long as we can. Only when we reach bottom is the return route open to us. This son rehearses every sentence he will say to his father, as if to memorize them. Then, at last, he heads for home.

That is the way it is with the people we like to point our fingers at, Christ says. Those are suffering people, the ones we call sinners: the prostitutes men stare at, despising and desiring them at the same time; hunted victims like the tax collectors we scorn, the poor bastards. That is how we should think of sin: not as temptation, but as misery; not as some kind of happiness that the pious don't enjoy, but as complete disaster.

We could ask whether this diagnosis of freedom betrayed is sufficient to enable us to understand the human tragedy, but at least it is a first and clearly comprehensible motive, a bridge to understanding. We must add that most of those who get into trouble do not have the kind of home Christ describes here. They do not have such a generous, understanding, open-hearted father. Instead, when they leap into the misery of their freedom as if it were their last chance at life, they do so to escape a real terror, a constant enslavement, a non-life at home, until in the end they themselves are guilty of going to the last extreme. They jump into life as they might jump through a window. Their misery and unhappiness needs to be painted much more fully in all its facets, but this much is enough to help us begin to see why Christ associated with prostitutes and tax collectors—in short, with sinners. He wanted to show a little bit, in his own life, of what the father in this story embodied. As soon as he sees his son, he forgets all his dignity and runs a long way to meet him. He interrupts the son's confession of guilt, embraces him, and has only one thought in mind: to wash away the shame and disgrace that are written in his clothes and in his whole bearing. A ring, shoes, a joyful feast: that is all he thinks about, and the Gospel could end there, except that at this point the people it is really addressing appear.

The older son comes from the field, and he is enraged by the music and feasting. In him, Christ paints the portrait of the pious, with full recognition and respect. This son is right. He has never violated a single law in his father's house, and in him there was not the tiniest bit of guilt or forgetfulness of his duty. That is how they all are—the pious, the Pharisees, the churchgoers—and yet their piety leads them to a worse temptation than the others' urge to freedom. Why is there so little freedom, joy, and understanding in the hearts of the good? Why do they see sin as a bit of happiness that has been stolen from them? The older brother has a very clear fantasy of the ways in which his younger brother must have spent his money. Nothing was said about it before, but the older son imagines it for us. He wasted his money on prostitutes, which is a very precise commentary. What he says is filled with a feeling of self-hatred for his own sense of being tempted, filled with his sadistic struggle against his own inclinations, as he sees them represented in the other's freedom. Piety is only self-repression, castration, mutilation, crushed happiness, a principle of cramping asceticism, petrifaction, and death. No one can love God that way, no matter how faithful one is. No one who feels that way can call God "Father," not even someone who sits in God's house every day.

There is only one proof that we love God: how ready and able we are to understand the needs of our own hearts and those of others. The pious and irreproachable have never known what despair is. They have no idea how helpless people can be. Is it really possible to learn understanding only through suffering, only through misery, only through tragedy? One would like to hope not, and yet it seems to be so. Should we believe that these words, the most beautiful ever spoken in all human history, were the last challenge to mutual understanding?

In Holy Week we will celebrate the consequences of these words. The older son learns not that one should return home where the music and dancing are, but rather that a man who speaks this way is eliminated, scourged, and crucified because of such a boundless love. That love creates so much anxiety, uncovers so much terror, that it releases a tide of inhumanity and evil in the hearts of those who appear to be on intimate terms with God and yet who only know the Lord God and never the Father, those who know the laws by heart but never know mercy. Ultimately, Christ could say the tax collectors and prostitutes know who God is. They are literally going into heaven before you, and in good Hebrew and plain English that means they are finding the way back to their Father, but you Pharisees are not.

These are words we all need to hear, if we know ourselves at all. May God forgive us our guilt and open our hearts to understand and forgive everyone, because that is how the Lord taught us to pray: Father, forgive us our sins as we are ready to forgive.

15. Drama or Tragedy?

Now there was a Pharisee named Nicodemus, a ruler of the Jews. He came to Jesus at night and said to him, "Rabbi, we know that you are a teacher who has come from God, for no one can do these signs that you are doing unless God is with him." Jesus answered and said to him, "Amen, amen, I say to you, no one can see the kingdom of God without being born from above." Nicodemus said to him, "How can a person once grown old be born again? Surely he cannot reenter his mother's womb and be born again, can he?" Jesus answered, "Amen, amen, I say to you, no one can enter the kingdom of God without being born of water and Spirit. What is born of flesh is flesh and what is born of spirit is spirit. Do not be amazed that I told you, 'You must be born from above.' The wind blows where it wills, and you can hear the sound it makes, but you do not know where it comes from or where it goes; so it is with everyone who is born of the Spirit." Nicodemus answered and said to him, "How can this happen?" Jesus answered and said to him, "You are the teacher of Israel and you do not understand this? Amen, amen, I say to you, we speak of what we know and we testify to what we have seen, but you people do not accept our testimony. If I tell you about earthly things and you do not believe, how will you believe if I tell you about heavenly things? No one has gone up to heaven except the one who has come down from heaven, the Son of Man. And just as Moses lifted up the serpent in the desert, so must the Son of Man be lifted up, so that everyone who believes in him may have eternal life."

For God so loved the world that he gave his only Son, so that everyone who believes in him might not perish but might have eternal life. For God did not send his Son into the world to condemn the world, but that the world might be saved through him. Whoever believes in him will not be condemned, but whoever does not believe has already been condemned, because he has not believed in the name of the only Son of God. And this is the verdict, that the light came into the world, but people preferred darkness to light, because their works were evil. For

everyone who does wicked things hates the light and does not
come toward the light, so that his works might not be exposed.
But whoever lives the truth comes to the light, so that his works
may be clearly seen as done in God (Jn 3:1-21).

Even when speaking of Jesus' death, the fourth Gospel remains
remarkably calm, composed, and elevated, like the altar painting in an
Eastern church, floating against a background of golden light. Even
though Jesus may have been deeply touched by suffering, the outcome
is already determined. This is the language of something already
established in the past: God has given the Son. It is only here, in the
third chapter, that the fourth Gospel begins to describe the life of Jesus,
but everything has already been decided long before, and the end is
fixed.

How is it possible to describe a human life in such a way that its
truth becomes clear? This is a question modern literature has repeatedly
posed for itself. About forty years ago there was a minor scandal in the
theatrical world when the French poet Jean Anouilh presented his
version of *Antigone*. It was quite different from what people had come
to expect. When we go to the theater and the curtain goes up, we expect
to be the witnesses of strange and dramatic events. We go to the theater
to be captured by events that are still unknown to us. We want our
feelings to be captivated as we hope, suffer, are disappointed, or rebel
along with the people in the play. That is the language of drama.
Anouilh took the stance of a sage, first sending a narrator onto the stage
to describe his anti-drama. The effect was as if one were to begin a
murder mystery by having the police captain describe the action in
advance and tell the solution as well. Where is the tension, then? we
ask. Anouilh's narrator explains that, unlike drama, tragedy is the true
place where life is at rest. The dice were thrown long since, and the
actors know it. If we are honest about it, we have known for a long time
how it is going to come out. All right, then, no more rebellion, no
kicking against the goad; instead, what we get is an exposition of what
is going on inside us.

That is just how the fourth Gospel intends its presentation of the life
of Jesus. Don't we know what people are like, and can't we guess how
they will react when a bright light from heaven falls on the darkness
and hopelessness in their world? Or rather, to look at it from God's
point of view, could we imagine that God would send God's own Son

into this world without having planned the gruesome finale ahead of time, or even having determined and staged it? The Johannine Jesus speaks like an insider, someone who not only knows God's plans but, as God's trusted messenger, reveals those plans and those willing to hear them into the circle of insiders. It is an image of a world in which everything is settled, a divine dramaturgy, a tragedy already complete. This way, and only this way, the story can keep from getting bogged down and can calmly say what is and what isn't, in a sweeping language that preserves the broad picture and holds everything in view.

However, this method and art of presentation has its own quirks, its limitations, and even its dangers. Can we really be unaffected witnesses to the death and suffering of Jesus, already relieved by faith from any necessity for decision? Is it really true, then, that people stand by prior decision on the side of light or of darkness, of good or of evil, and all that matters is to make the division public? Something rebels in us if we are asked to apply this divine determination to ourselves. We don't want to be like that, and yet we have to acknowledge that it seems to be that way, in large measure. But we have to bring down this order of laws by which everything is determined from heaven to earth, from the throne of God to the realm in which God truly rules, in our own hearts. Then we can understand John very well. There are people who avoid the light. It would seem that we would long for nothing so much as salvation, but when it comes it is so hard for us to grasp it, almost harder than flinging ourselves repeatedly against the dark walls of our prison. The motives for this that Jesus names in his conversation with Nicodemus are, in fact, shame and fear. It can happen that we have already done so many things wrong and have trapped ourselves so completely in the net of our own lies and mistakes that in a certain sense it is the remnants of our ego that keep us from being freed. It can happen that we are so much identified with the negatives that we ultimately invest our pride in something that clearly makes no sense, and we assert our dignity and advertise our better nature precisely at the points where we have the least right to do so. In simpler terms: it can happen that we become like bats, night-flying creatures who are so accustomed to the dark that our whole biorhythm is attuned to these shadowy periods, as if our eyes would be hurt and our whole lives would have to be turned inside out if we were dragged out of our caves and the hidden and fearful forms of our existence were exposed to the quiet regions of light and the brightness of day.

But that is just what Jesus asks of us. He wants us to stop stamping down our own longing for a life of brightness, joy and happiness, to let go of everything that to this point has seemed to us at least worth defending, perhaps even great and a source of pride, and learn to live quite simply. Of course, this simple truth seems dreadful to us at first. The little bit of trust we can learn here urges us to give up all our insurance against fear. The little bit of joy we can acquire urges us to let go of the security of resignation. In all these points we have to learn to cross these borderlands of uncertainty as we might cross a bridge between two shores to enter another world that belongs to God and in which security is no longer achieved with walls and armor, but through trust. Then we would pass from darkness to light, from torture to happiness, from death to life.

That, Jesus tells us, is what God really wants. God does not send the Son into the world with his message of reconciliation in order to judge the world, and yet the judgment on the life of every individual consists in the extent to which that person accepts and understands the message. As soon as we begin to talk of judgment, we hear the hard language that can be derived from John and that so often creates misunderstanding: talk about right thinking, training, correcting, executing. If this message of Jesus appears in the world as judgment, then it is as an honest offer to allow us to set ourselves right, to be honest with ourselves. In honesty and uprightness we can get through this world, not twisted, martyred, and obsessed, ready to torture what could save us and kill that from which we truly live. It seems as if it *must* be that way. John thinks that Jesus saw it that way from the beginning and accepted it for himself, believing that God also wanted it that way. In reality, what God wants is not the terror of anxiety and the tyranny of false shame; God desires that we should live.

Fifth Sunday of Lent

16. Something New

Thus says the Lord,
*   who opens a way in the sea*
*   and a path in the mighty waters,*
Who leads out chariots and horsemen,
*   a powerful army,*
Till they lie prostrate together, never to rise,
*   snuffed out and quenched like a wick.*
Remember not the events of the past,
*   the things of long ago consider not;*
See, I am doing something new!
*   Now it springs forth, do you not perceive it?*
In the desert I make a way,
*   in the wasteland, rivers.*
Wild beasts honor me,
*   jackals and ostriches,*
For I put water in the desert
*   and rivers in the wasteland*
*   for my chosen people to drink,*

The people whom I formed for myself,
that they might announce my praise (Is 43:16-21).

The usual prescription for hopelessness is courage, and for sadness, optimism. But it frequently happens that our courage depends on the state of our nerves, and our optimism on our mood. When our existence is really jeopardized, neither courage nor optimism quite fills the bill.

The man we call Second Isaiah was placed in just such a perilous situation. He had to respond to a catastrophe affecting his people, similar to the one that had happened two hundred years earlier when the Assyrians snapped up Israel like a sitting duck. This time it was still worse: Disaster fell on the tiny remnant nation of Juda and its capital, Jerusalem. The Babylonians had destroyed the Temple, left the city in ruins, and marched the chosen people away into exile. The people of Israel were scattered over the mountains and hills of the land like sheep without a shepherd. They had not just been robbed of something, but in fact of everything in which they had fixed their hopes. The tragedy of this people is, in essence, a catastrophe of faith, for it seems that God either will not or cannot help God's people against the stronger power of the Babylonians. And in whom had they really placed their trust, with all their prayers and sacrifices?

Every individual life will have many such hours in which it seems everything we have relied on has been destroyed. Yet it all seemed to have been God's gift; it seemed reliable and certain. Now is it all nothing because the powers from outside and fear and helplessness within are evidently mightier? What can we say in this hour of despair? This prophet makes an attempt by recalling a scene from the past, an hour that appeared just as hopeless, when Israel was flying before the chariots of the Egyptians, fleeing toward freedom. The Red Sea barred their way, and they did not know which way to turn. They could not go forward through the water, and the road was blocked behind them. It was Moses who, in unshaken trust, stretched his hand over the water and opened a way where there was none. In fact, it was only through just such powerful trust in the face of all appearances that it was possible to go farther, and if there had not been such hours, and many of them, we would not be where we are today.

Someone may object that the days of King Nebuchadnezzar are not those of Moses. History does not repeat itself, and the things that were do not happen again. What kind of hope can be founded on the past?

But this prophet, whose name we do not know and whose message of hope nevertheless echoes through millennia, would stubbornly and keenly ask again: In that case, what kind of despair can be founded on nothing but the evidence of what has been? The more desperate we are, the more it grabs us by the shoulders and turns us backward, forcing our thoughts farther and farther into the past. Everything seems dark there, like a single great proof that there is no way out and no hope. Yet there are also those undeniable moments in every human life when hope conquers fear, or else we would never dare to live. These two things, the evidence of happiness and the evidence of pain, could neutralize each other, or at least it would be something gained if we could see in the agents of our fear something like messengers of God, as if God had actually sent Pharaoh's chariots in order to destroy them once and for all. In fact, that is what the prophet says, not on his own initiative, as a human suggestion, but as a message from God. "Thus says the Lord: remember not the events of the past, the things of long ago consider not." At some point we can draw a line under the sufferings of the past; they are finished. We can lift our eyes to the future, and in the midst of suffering we can sense the beginning of something new. New seed sprouts in the scorched earth, new shoots and stalks push upward, and life unfolds toward the future. It is our same old life, not completely different, and yet in the space created by hope and confidence we become new people, no longer subject to fear, helplessness, and despair, but open to hope, capable of happiness, ripe for joy.

We have to keep these desert experiences before our eyes, because again and again, in the midst of suffering, we will feel like people collapsing out of sheer longing, wandering about within the horizon of a constant *fata morgana,* and we can no longer believe in anything for fear of being disappointed. We have to look at the animals: the jackal, the ostrich, the antelope. When the desert and steppe are dry, they stand with open mouths and in their longing for water try to drink the hot air while the parching heat dries their mouths and throats even more mercilessly. When the lakes dry up the water birds fly into the desert seeking new sources of water; they even leave their young, who do not understand how there can be nothing but burning sand where a few days before there were lakes and ponds. But then within a few hours clouds can appear in the west, crowd up over the desert and darken the sun, and strong, driving rain breaks over the earth. In those hours a joyful, exuberant life explodes in the desert. The antelope jump high in the air, and the ostriches swirl in their delirious dance. They do not know or care that in a few months the dry weather will return and death will stalk them again.

Nature expects nothing else but an equal measure of coming and going, appearing and disappearing, life and death. But God has made us humans in such a way that we step out of that equal rhythm and again and again throw a measure of hope into the scales of life, in spite of all the earthly experiences we know so well. This tiny gram of hope tips the scale and lets our life go on, even here on earth. For the message remains and cannot be shaken. Each of us can and should think like Israel, taught by the wonderful unknown prophet in the Babylonian exile: We are and always will be God's chosen ones. God is not finished with us. We are in the hand of God, and God will never let us go, will never leave us. We are God's own possession, and God will protect us, no matter what happens. However narrow our life seems, however powerless we are, however rootless, we remain God's possession in time and eternity.

17. Who Will Condemn?

Jesus went to the Mount of Olives. But early in the morning he arrived again in the temple area, and all the people started coming to him, and he sat down and taught them. Then the scribes and the Pharisees brought a woman who had been caught in adultery and made her stand in the middle. They said to him, "Teacher, this woman was caught in the very act of committing adultery. Now in the law, Moses commanded us to stone such women. So what do you say?" They said this to test him, so that they could have some charge to bring against him. Jesus bent down and began to write on the ground with his finger. But when they continued asking him, he straightened up and said to them, "Let the one among you who is without sin be the first to throw a stone at her." Again he bent down and wrote on the ground.

*And in response, they went away one by one, beginning with the
elders. So he was left alone with the woman before him. Then
Jesus straightened up and said to her, "Woman, where are they?
Has no one condemned you?" She replied, "No one, sir." Then
Jesus said, "Neither do I condemn you. Go, [and] from now on
do not sin any more" (Jn 8:1-11).*

From the earliest days of the Church until today, this little story has
made great difficulty for theologians. Can it be true that Jesus could
have let a woman guilty of such a terrible sin as adultery, and deserving
to be punished, simply go free without even a warning, with no clear
determination of guilt, totally unpunished? Doesn't such behavior rock
the solid foundations of the law and the civil order? It took almost a
hundred years, during the time when the New Testament was being
composed and collected, for people to integrate this story into the life
of Jesus as told in the sacred texts. For that reason it was shoved into
the fourth Gospel, the last one written, at a very late stage. Looking
back on it all, we have to say, thank God.

In the gospel stories we read of many miracles Jesus did because he
had power over human hearts. But there is scarcely any other story that
so amazingly shows how, on a certain morning in the court of the
Temple in Jerusalem, Jesus was able to transform a group of people
from the inside out. Because the story is in the New Testament, two
Christian groups in particular have adopted this story as their own.

The Christian Pharisees, having gnashed their teeth at first, finally
grit them and say that this is really *their* story, because, after all, it ends
with Jesus telling the sinful woman not to sin any more. So the world
is in order again, and everything in between is nothing but a brief
shudder like a small earthquake that can easily be forgotten once we
have repaired the cracks in the walls. To tell the truth, this story is the
ongoing center of an earthquake that will never stop; it is an unsettling
event that shakes us down to our toes. Nothing is "all right" if the
human heart is as monstrous as it appears to Jesus here and as
magnificent as he trusts that it can be. After reading a text like this, it
is impossible to return contentedly to the world of legalists and law-
givers.

On the other hand, the story is very popular with those who are
interested in changing the social order. Is it not true that this whole
scenario is only possible in an extremely patriarchal society? A woman

is caught in adultery, but not the man who did it with her. The men are standing around with stones in their hands, but women are the defenseless victims of this kind of legal practice that only affects the helpless. Does this not correspond in every detail to the masculine macho-mentality, even now? Seducing a woman is a deed of honor, in some sense even an obligation for brave men, but the woman a man marries must, of course, be absolutely pure. We can certainly call that a masculine double standard, and in any case it is an exercise of violence on the part of the powerful. We are right to be outraged and angry about it. In Jesus' time there was someone who wanted to take the part of the defenseless women, but in doing so he illustrated what separated him from Jesus. Forty years after Jesus, after the destruction of Jerusalem, Rabbi Johanan Ben Zacchai pursued the same intention, but in a very different way. He solved the problem of adultery and the condemnation of women through legal interpretation. Taking a passage from the prophet Amos that calls Israel an adulterous nation (by which the prophet meant that no one in the chosen people was innocent of having broken faith with God), the Jewish rabbi read it to mean that no man could have the right to pass judgment on adultery because he himself was guilty of the same sin. The Pharisees eased the severity of the law by applying the law.

In both cases the lawgiver requires a certain power status, and in any case it is a kind of politics, perhaps more just and more humane, but still politics. That is the crux of this story at the beginning. The people who literally throw this woman into Jesus' arms really have no interest in her as a person. They simply use her as a pawn on behalf of their own interests: namely, they want to get at Jesus in some way, to trap him and drive him into a corner. If what he says is true, that "God lets the sun shine on the good and the evil alike," as if it didn't matter, if his parables about a God who forgives just because we need it are to be taken seriously, isn't he saying that a clear definition of morality is null and void? If that is what he means, he is obviously putting himself in opposition to the holiest thing in Israel, the law of Moses; and if he is doing that, he ought to own up to it and pay the price. Or maybe he will be afraid of the consequences of his own talk, and then people can rightly say of him that he is nothing but a Sunday preacher and a charlatan. If he holds with Moses, everything he has been saying is false, and then he is even more thoroughly finished. In one case he will be exposed as a man of character, but an anarchist, and in the other case he is a reed in the wind with no authority at all. He is in a trap, just as they hoped, and to spring the trap they need another person. That is the principle of politics: You have to make people into pawns or dominos for the game. Then you set up the whole game so as to tie up the opponent, tighter and tighter, and if you can succeed in handling people that way, you can console yourself with the thought that you are doing it all for their benefit. But do people faced with such hurdles set up by established interests really get a turn of their own, and when can we allow ourselves to be concerned with the interests of people for their own sake? But the problem is much deeper and more a matter of principle. As long as we are thinking only of other people, we have some clear ideas about what to do. We have to exhibit responsibility, sympathy, care, and Christian charity; then we are good, upright people and always in the position of being better and stronger, those who have something to give, and that is extremely flattering to our self-concept. Heaven holds its breath for an instant when Jesus fails to respond to the question: "What do you say?" Instead, he bends down and writes in the sand. The exegetes have been scratching their heads for centuries over the question of what Jesus could have written. But it is not a question of what he was writing; everything that could be written is at stake here. There is a lot in the books of the law, but does being written on parchment or paper make it more valid than something we would entrust to the sand, where one gust of wind would wipe it away so that it could never be read again? None of it is really enduring; what could and must be valid is what God has written in our hearts. What would we see if we began to understand ourselves?

On that morning in the Temple court, there happened what may well have been the greatest miracle Jesus worked. People who were unaware of being guilty of anything, people who were standing there on behalf of the good, ready to defend it with the instruments of punishment they held in their hands, were convinced that instead of looking outward to judge, they should look inward for the reasons why human beings do things. The whole world is changed. No matter how reasonable or how stupid the laws may be, it is what we as human beings are that determines how we apply them. Everything is decided in our hearts, and nothing but the power of understanding is able to call people into freedom. Apparently Jesus' opponents in today's Gospel resist this idea for a long time, until finally Jesus stands up in anger and flings a challenge at them: "Let the one among you who is without sin be the first to throw a stone at her!" This scene was masterfully portrayed in a recent film. Jesus takes the stones in his own hands, clashes them wrathfully together, and holds them under the noses of his opponents, the defenders of good order and law. "Here, throw them!" he shouts at them. If there had been just one who was absolutely solid in his self-confidence, Jesus could not have prevented this legal murder, or rather, the execution of justice as prescribed by law. Let the one without sin cast the first stone.

It may be easy to listen to Jesus saying, in the Sermon on the Mount, "stop judging, that you may not be judged," but to summon the strength to act that way in a moment of extreme challenge is almost beyond human ability. They start to leave, the elders among the first. We can scarcely believe our ears when we hear that at the end Jesus does not exclude himself from the group of people who came to give judgment. "Has no one condemned you?" he asks the woman, standing up again. And when she replies, "No one, sir," Jesus says: "Then neither do I condemn you." This is the end of the parties we establish when we separate people into good and bad; it is the end of moral absolutes and clear, cast-iron concepts; in particular, it is the end of the prejudices that tell us how things ought to be in other people's lives and how it will be with us, too, tomorrow and the day after. The Christian Pharisees like to cling to the final sentence: "Go, [and] from now on do not sin any more." But they are translating it badly. Hebrew is a tricky language. For the imperative it normally uses the future tense, so that we would have to read this as: "Now you go, and in the future you will not sin." That is not a command, but rather the assurance of a fact. The whole art of things is to bring people to the point where, when they have lost all their external security, they can feel secure in their own hearts, as far as that is possible. To restore so much inner harmony and sense in the soul of a devastated human being, after the whole of that person's self-confidence has been shattered, is the second miracle in this story, and it is almost greater than the first, so great that in our own lives it can take years to accomplish. Incidentally, the story leaves open the question of how this woman's life will look in the future.

We may feel disoriented by this story, so let me make a practical application. We are living in a time when, of 300,000 marriages entered into in Germany in a given year, a third will be dissolved, and that is only a drop in the bucket. In Canada 40 percent of marriages end in divorce, and in the United States it is one out of every two. It is useless to think that all this is only the consequence of infidelity, the decline of morals, or unbounded sexuality, as we read in so many Church pronouncements. In reality it is often a cry of profound suffering and a desperate search for love. Along the way—I say this as a priest—I see and hear a great deal about adultery, and I must admit that I can no longer say definitely "this is wrong and this is right," simply because many people really cannot regret what they have done. They are sorry about it, it causes them pain, of course, but when something is not just an adventure, something you can excuse the next morning because you had drunk too much the night before, when something spiritual has really happened, something that touches us deeply, then we are not in a position to judge ourselves by saying, "this is right, this is wrong, and starting tomorrow I will change."

Shall I say that I know of adulteries that have healed women who had previously suffered from psychosomatic illnesses, and no one could cure them, neither their husbands nor their psychiatrists nor their doctors, but a vacation encounter accomplished it, and the healing was a lasting one? Could it not be that there are women who, after years of degradation in their marriages, meet some man in a spa or vacation hotel who can restore to them a little of their dignity and a certain sense of their lost dreams? Could it not be that we must sometimes walk on what appear to be crooked paths in order to find what is essential and right for us? And how many marriages are like closed fortresses, bastions under siege that only endure because now and then a carrier pigeon flutters in? What do we know, and what can we lay down as certain about human beings, just because we are in possession of certain books? And what are we doing in the Church, when we ignore the questions of nuclear war and weapons, environmental poisoning and destruction, the daily extermination of species, and fixate on the subject of marriage, producing every conceivable kind of declaration, rule of punishment, and definition of what is permissible before marriage, in marriage, after marriage? Let the one among us who is without sin cast the first stone! On the other hand, anyone who is able to touch human beings from within so that they can confidently say they have put the past behind them is very close to Jesus. There is a world of difference between the two.

18. Come Forth

Now a man was ill, Lazarus from Bethany, the village of Mary
and her sister Martha. Mary was the one who had anointed the
Lord with perfumed oil and dried his feet with her hair; it was
her brother Lazarus who was ill. So the sisters sent word to him,
saying, "Master, the one you love is ill." When Jesus heard this
he said, "This illness is not to end in death, but is for the glory
of God, that the Son of God may be glorified through it." Now
Jesus loved Martha and her sister and Lazarus. So when he heard
that he was ill, he remained for two days in the place where he
was. Then after this he said to his disciples, "Let us go back to
Judea." The disciples said to him, "Rabbi, the Jews were just
trying to stone you, and you want to go back there?" Jesus
answered, "Are there not twelve hours in a day? If one walks
during the day, he does not stumble, because he sees the light of
this world. But if one walks at night, he stumbles, because the
light is not in him." He said this, and then told them, "Our friend
Lazarus is asleep, but I am going to awaken him." So the
disciples said to him, "Master, if he is asleep, he will be saved."
But Jesus was talking about his death, while they thought that he
meant ordinary sleep. So then Jesus said to them clearly,
"Lazarus has died. And I am glad for you that I was not there,
that you may believe. Let us go to him." So Thomas, called
Didymus, said to his fellow disciples, "Let us also go to die with
him."

When Jesus arrived, he found that Lazarus had already been
in the tomb for four days. Now Bethany was near Jerusalem, only
about two miles away. And many of the Jews had come to Martha
and Mary to comfort them about their brother. When Martha
heard that Jesus was coming, she went to meet him; but Mary sat
at home. Martha said to Jesus, "Lord, if you had been here, my
brother would not have died. [But] even now I know that whatever you ask of God, God will give you." Jesus said to her, "Your
brother will rise." Martha said to him, "I know he will rise, in
the resurrection on the last day." Jesus told her, "I am the
resurrection and the life; all those who believe in me, even if they

die, will live, and everyone who lives and believes in me will never die. Do you believe this?" She said to him, "Yes, Lord. I have come to believe that you are the Messiah, the Son of God, the one who is coming into the world."

When she had said this, she went and called her sister Mary secretly, saying, "The teacher is here and is asking for you." As soon as she heard this, she rose quickly and went to him. For Jesus had not yet come into the village, but was still where Martha had met him. So when the Jews who were with her in the house comforting her saw Mary get up quickly and go out, they followed her, presuming that she was going to the tomb to weep there. When Mary came to where Jesus was and saw him, she fell at his feet and said to him, "Lord, if you had been here, my brother would not have died." When Jesus saw her weeping and the Jews who had come with her weeping, he became perturbed and deeply troubled, and said, "Where have you laid him?" They said to him, "Sir, come and see." And Jesus wept. So the Jews said, "See how he loved him." But some of them said, "Could not the one who opened the eyes of the blind man have done something so that this man would not have died?"

So Jesus, perturbed again, came to the tomb. It was a cave, and a stone lay across it. Jesus said, "Take away the stone." Martha, the dead man's sister, said to him, "Lord, by now there will be a stench; he has been dead for four days." Jesus said to her, "Did I not tell you that if you believe you will see the glory of God?" So they took away the stone. And Jesus raised his eyes and said, "Father, I thank you for hearing me. I know that you always hear me; but because of the crowd here I have said this, that they may believe that you sent me." And when he had said this, he cried out in a loud voice, "Lazarus, come out!" The dead man came out, tied hand and foot with burial bands, and his face was wrapped in a cloth. So Jesus said to them, "Untie him and let him go" (Jn 11:1-45).

Of all the images the fourth Gospel uses to describe the process of conviction, the path to faith in Jesus as the Son of God, the most radical and consoling is this last one, the raising of Lazarus, which comes immediately before the narrative of the death and resurrection of Jesus himself.

Experiencing God, as Jesus explains in the third chapter of this Gospel, in his midnight dialogue with the counselor Nicodemus, is like being born anew in the power of the Spirit. As though fetters that had been binding us were cut away, our soul is free and seems as if borne by the power of the wind, incalculable, beyond all limits, only following the breath of God into endless distances. This miracle can happen: to be given oneself anew and to begin life all over again, as if heaven descended to earth.

As Jesus shows the man born blind in the ninth chapter of John's Gospel, experiencing God, as God appears in Christ, is like having our eyes opened after gazing always on an endless night. Year after year, our life can be imprisoned in hopelessness and crushed by blindness. Yet it is possible, by a kind of rebirth, to wash our eyes in the pool of Siloam and to see the world in a completely new way. The keepers of the law will object and debate whether this view of the world is genuine and permissible, but there are evidences of humanity that cannot be obliterated once we begin really to *see*.

The story of the raising of Lazarus is the summary of all these images. Experiencing God means moving from death to life and overcoming the sickness of despair, decay, and eternal imprisonment in the walled dungeon of the grave. When the linen bands fall away and we emerge into the light, following the call of God, "Lazarus, come forth!" the womb of the earth will no longer be able to hold us prisoners, and we will be free.

A hundred years ago the Russian writer Fyodor Dostoyevski placed this story of the raising of Lazarus at the center of one of his greatest novels, *Crime and Punishment*. Somewhere in St. Petersburg lives a young man who could have his whole life before him, a gifted genius, an extraordinary intellect, destined for greatness. But he huddles in his room and spends his days idly lying on his cot, staring at the ceiling and brooding. He is torn by self-doubt and the bitterest self-hatred, yet at the same time he craves renown to the point of madness. He can come to terms neither with himself nor with anyone else. In his bitterness and malice he manages to quarrel with his last friend. He is tortured by poverty and oppressed by suffering, and in the night he sees himself multiplied and sinking in a sea of vermin. For that is what he thinks of himself: He is something completely worthless, something it would almost be right to tread underfoot. His is a life between death, madness, and murder: what we call despair, the one sickness that is really unto death. Dostoyevski contrasts him with the figure of a girl, a prostitute who takes to the streets to preserve her family from utter ruin. This man, the student and murderer Rodion Raskolnikov, meets the girl. When he understands her situation, he sees only three possibilities for Sonia: she will accommodate herself to all this disgusting filth, or she will go completely mad, or she will take her own life. But Sonia does none of these things because she has a secret she hesitates to share. Finally, when Rodion presses her for a long time, she opens her Bible and together the prostitute and the murderer read the story of the raising of Lazarus and how Jesus says to him, "Lazarus, come forth!"

It is possible for people who have never seen the light of this world to dare to believe that this call is addressed to them. It is possible that the feeling of decaying within one's own living body, because the soul cannot sustain such an existence, can be overcome by the call of love. It is possible for a life that seems destined only for death to receive a glimpse of eternity. For the fourth Gospel, it is of the highest importance that we should not believe in the resurrection as a distant, foreign event at the end of time. There could never have been an Easter morning, and even if it had happened we could never have known it, were it not that we are able in the midst of this life to experience God in such a way that we understand what life is: beyond the fear of death, beyond mortality, beyond the narrowness and anxieties of this world. This call, "come forth!" is for us today, no matter where we are. Whether you are twenty, or forty, or sixty years old—it is never too early and never too late to feel, to see, and to hear that there are not two worlds, this one and the one beyond, separated in time and in their essential nature. The God of Jesus Christ is present today; God's presence is eternal. That is our whole life: to believe and to know that there are no barriers between earth and heaven, between time and eternity, between humanity and divinity; that there is only a single realm of love and life, to which we are called.

19. Life Without Fear

Now there were some Greeks among those who had come up to worship at the feast. They came to Philip, who was from Bethsaida in Galilee, and asked him, "Sir, we would like to see Jesus." Philip went and told Andrew; then Andrew and Philip went and told Jesus. Jesus answered them, "The hour has come for the Son of Man to be glorified. Amen, amen, I say to you, unless a grain of wheat falls to the ground and dies, it remains just a grain of wheat; but if it dies, it produces much fruit. Whoever loves his life loses it, and whoever hates his life in this world will preserve it for eternal life. Whoever serves me must follow me, and where I am, there also will my servant be. The Father will honor whoever serves me.

"I am troubled now. Yet what should I say? 'Father, save me from this hour'? But it was for this purpose that I came to this hour. Father, glorify your name." Then a voice came from heaven, "I have glorified it and will glorify it again." The crowd there heard it and said it was thunder; but others said, "An angel has spoken to him." Jesus answered and said, "This voice did not come for my sake but for yours. Now is the time of judgment on this world; now the ruler of this world will be driven out. And when I am lifted up from the earth, I will draw everyone to myself." He said this indicating the kind of death he would die (Jn 12:20-33).

For two thousand years, people from the most varied cultures have been coming to Jesus' disciples and saying: "We would like to see the Lord," and through the people who believe in Christ, they acquire an insight into the nature and the teaching of Christ.

Today's Gospel, placed immediately before the beginning of the celebration of the Lord's passion, attempts to sum up the mystery of Jesus' life and death in his own words. It is a moment in which Christ himself says that he is deeply distressed at the thought of his certain death, that he is shaken by fear. But the question arises: How does anyone live in the face of death?

Now and then one has the impression that immortal life is something one can choose to believe in or not. It seems as if it would scarcely make any difference which one believed. This apparent situation is shattered, first of all, by the words of this Gospel. All eternity depends on what we really believe. But we can test this now, in an instant, because with every breath we *are* different, we exist differently, we are different people according to what we believe, and in essence that means according to the way we confront death. Jesus dares to accept the final challenge of his life and not to avoid it. Therefore we can and must say that he died for us. For what was revealed in him became, in his death, a message that opens graves and deprives death of its fearfulness. What should Jesus have said? "Father, save me from this hour"? "But," he adds, "it was for this purpose that I came to this hour," namely so that this world could finally be brought to a decision. As long as we think that we have to defend our earthly life with teeth and claws, our life will shrink together and become an ever-narrower tomb. Fear of death will kill us long before its physical occurrence. The power of genuine existence, the ability to breathe deeply, will be taken from us as we engage in the increasingly hectic and choking quest, not to live, but to make our lives secure, to undergird and insure and reinsure them, and the more dead certain they are, the more certainly are they dead. We need to let the screaming contrast found at this point in the Gospel strike us with its full force, as Jesus uses a Hebrew contrast to say as bluntly as possible: "Those who love this life will lose it. Only those who hate this life, this earthly life, their own life, will save it for all eternity." We can only translate this in such a way as to show that as far as Jesus is concerned, it is a matter of complete indifference how long we live, how securely we live, how apparently successful we are, and how we preserve what is called a successful life. Those who start that way will never get to the essential core, will never find themselves, and in the grave they dig for themselves they can neither believe in nor even desire eternity.

But something else is at stake here: that we should lose our fear of being in the wrong. Death is not the ultimate power in our life. Why did Jesus come to this hour, if not because he wanted to teach and embody the truth that it is possible to endure fear and still be human, openhearted, and generous, abandoning all security? That bothered everybody. He made people nervous, and so he brought out all their defenses and countermeasures against fear. But he had to stick to his position. For the sake of our humanity, he had, for once, to open up the walls that constrict and choke us and affirm that truth is more important than the question of how it is received, that it is worth more to live as a human being than to accept lazy compromises. Then it works. It is possible that every word we say about goodness and humanity will be twisted and interpreted differently from what we mean. In the end the righteous will stand there and say that we have only made a mess, created chaos, and upset the order of things. We certainly have done that. It is possible that with every step we take toward truth and humanity we are being led on, that we are becoming defenseless victims, that we will be pilloried and destroyed. But Jesus knew that, and he wanted to show us once and for all that it may be terrible to be calumniated, led out naked, beaten, and tortured to death, but none of that is worse than denying our own life every day, shaming and dirtying it and delivering it up to the death of fear. We owe it to ourselves and to the God who made us to believe in the glory of life—of every human life including our own—to do away with the worship of false gods, and to face life worthily and proudly. A human being who is free is the greatest glory of God, and that is what Jesus prays for. That is his desire: to enable people to live transparently and in clarity before their Creator.

Then a voice from heaven is heard, and the question arises: What do we hear? We can see the world as it appears around us. Then facts are facts and things are things, our body is only a body and our life is more or less a combined response to natural laws. Then our contact with heaven will consist of knowing that it thunders or rains on us, and the wind blows, and sometime or other we will sink down into the ground. Or we can learn a new way of looking at the world. Then it is a matter of hearing, in the midst of life, how an angel of God speaks with every one of us. Then what is at stake is understanding this life as an eternal mystery that we slowly understand, and the more deeply we understand it, the more fascinating, unfathomable, and heavenly we find it to be. For the truth is that this life of ours is made up of a never-ending conversation between here and there, between earth and heaven, between the finite and the infinite, and the angel of God is always speaking to us.

Then there is this image of the grain of wheat that falls into the ground. If we take it biologically, it is the bitterest thing we can say. We would be nothing but a part of nature, with a passing existence that is quickly ended, and soon the balance will show that the best thing we can do is to make room for those who come after us and not stand in their way. But if we take it as a living image, as something about heaven, the grain of wheat can teach us how to live. We ourselves, with our tiny, vulnerable, narrow existence, have infinitely much to give each other. Every little bit of love that we can produce for one another in the face of fear makes us the bread of heaven, the pilgrims' food on the journey to the infinite future.

The truth is that there really is no such thing as death, but there is a brotherly and sisterly existence that begins here on earth and never ends. This is the question that determines everything; this decides what we really believe in: this world—and the fourth Gospel does not hesitate to call it the devil—or God. If we believe in God, heaven is close to us. As far as externals are concerned, we can ask what difference it makes whether we believe in the one or the other: Biologically, all of us are going to die. But this question is decisive for our whole life and for the whole world! The disciples could have said to Jesus, "But you are going to die!" And Jesus would have had to answer them at this point, "Yes, for that very reason I am going to die, and this is glory, because to die in this way denies nothing of the truth, but instead confirms it and destroys forever the power of narrowness and the clinging to what is here and now." On the other hand, Jesus could have succumbed to fear and preserved his life for a decade or two, but it would not have been life anymore. It would have been nothing but a pitiful disgrace. As it is, it remains forever something praiseworthy, great, and glorious that gives us a hint of our calling for all eternity. We do not need to shrink back any more in face of the idols and puppets that are set up before us. We experience the paradox that death is less fearful, in some circumstances, than the people around us: for children these may be their own parents, for adults other, apparently bigger adults. But we need no longer fear if we know what we are in the eyes of God, if we see ourselves and our lives through the words of Jesus in this Gospel. The crucifixion is the beginning of glory and the cross a flowering tree, an axis between heaven and earth, and the voice from heaven will remain with us, assuring us that God loves us forever and that together we will never fall out of that love.

✟ Palm Sunday

20. How Can This Happen?

Scriptural Reading: Matthew 26-27

The narrative of the passion of our Lord Jesus Christ that we hear read today in the Gospel according to Matthew is not really a description of historical events. Matthew, closely following the Gospel of Mark, describes the passion of Jesus as a prayer that develops in a series of steps as the culmination of the promises of the old covenant and as the will of God that is now finally brought to fulfillment. Behind all this we can discern the traces of what is often a simpler truth, the human situation. According to Matthew, Jesus dies because he has admitted before the High Priest that he is the Son of God, the Son of Man who will come with the clouds of heaven. We can inquire, on the historical plane, whether such a trial before Caiaphas ever took place, but it is certain that Jesus never made such an admission.

The story of the passion begins with the institution of the Lord's Supper, when Jesus gives himself to his disciples as food and drink under the forms of bread and wine. But it must all have begun with Jesus' simple invitation to all those people who, in the minds of the scribes and high priests, had no chance to return to God: the tax collectors, the sinners, the prostitutes. He wanted to gather them together, to sit down with them, so that a little of heaven would come to earth just for them. The whole thing must have been moving toward its crucial moment when Jesus went up to Jerusalem to open the Temple at the head of this group that joined him and at his side found confidence in God and in the validity of their own existence. "My house shall be called a house of prayer for all peoples." With the words of Third Isaiah, Jesus asks that the sanctuary should not be barred to Gentiles, women, those who appear to be unworthy. God's world is open, just as it shows itself between sunrise and sunset, an unconditional mercy and goodness that includes everyone. That is the real reason he was rejected by the high priests, the scribes, and the elders. Matthew's Gospel deliberately attributes a lot of things to them: Confession of Jesus Christ was often used in the early Church as an accusation against the synagogue, and so we see the evangelist describing how this group intrigues among the people during Jesus' trial until they themselves declare the king of Israel guilty before the seat of the governor, Pontius Pilate.

The simpler truth that underlies the description of Jesus' passion is that the behavior of all the people who appear there is contrary to their real desire. Peter does *not* want to betray his Lord, but that is just what he will do, for fear of a maidservant. Judas appears to hand over his Lord for a despicable sum of money, but he really wants to save him, as his later words show. He thinks he is not guilty, and his strange tactics are apparently intended to force Jesus and his accusers to come to some agreement. He wants to compromise instead of deciding. Peter himself, in the scene of Jesus' arrest in the garden, grabs his sword, but Jesus does not want violence to win. As he explains, everyone who takes the sword will perish by the sword. And is Pilate to be envied his powerful role? He is really powerless, the people's football, and the rulers themselves are obedient and submissive to the will of the ruled. None of the people in this story do or say what they really think, except for the women. Only in Matthew's Gospel do we read that Pilate's wife intervened. She had a dream that warned her. But when do people listen to dreams, especially from women? So it all ends with the group of women receiving Jesus after he had been killed and carrying him to the grave as the last service of their love.

The question remains for us: What next? Matthew describes the death of Jesus as the beginning of an earthquake. There is no more foundation, no more security, if it is possible to kill *him,* who at least for the group of women was the beginning of life. The graves will open, and what people call "dead" begins to live. In turn people will learn that what was formerly called "life" is nothing but an endless practice of death. It is possible to seal a grave, and even to set a watch over it, but no one can put a stop to the life that begins in those who have understood it all.

Holy Thursday

21. A New Covenant

When the hour came, he took his place at table with the apostles. He said to them, "I have eagerly desired to eat this Passover with you before I suffer, for, I tell you, I shall not eat it [again] until there is fulfillment in the kingdom of God." Then he took a cup, gave thanks, and said, "Take this and share it among yourselves; for I tell you [that] from this time on I shall not drink of the fruit of the vine until the kingdom of God comes." Then he took the bread, said the blessing, broke it, and gave it to them, saying, "This is my body, which will be given for you; do this in memory of me." And likewise the cup after they had eaten, saying, "This cup is the new covenant in my blood, which will be shed for you. And yet behold, the hand of the one who is to betray me is with me on the table; for the Son of Man indeed goes as it has been determined; but woe to that man by whom he is betrayed." And they began to debate among themselves who among them would do such a deed (Lk 22:14-23).

The scene in the upper room, when Jesus reclines at table with his disciples, is the beginning of his passion. The Sanhedrin has already given its verdict against him; all that remains is to pass the death sentence. The betrayer himself is sitting at the same table, and Jesus knows it; he desires nothing else but the suffering that awaits him in this night. There seems to be no other way.

This man who has been ejected from the synagogue must celebrate the ancestral meal on this evening without the ritually prescribed paschal lamb. But is a sacrificial animal necessary? What was the answer to Isaac's question to his father at Mount Moriah: "Here are the fire and the wood, but where is the sheep for the holocaust?" Abraham had no answer to give him. At this hour, Jesus knows the answer; the only question is when his disciples will understand what is really happening and when we ourselves will understand it, thousands of years later. Using the texts of the Passover liturgy, Jesus takes bread in his hands and prays, in the language of his native Galilee, the words prescribed: "This is the bread of suffering that our ancestors ate in a foreign land. Let all who are hungry come to the Passover meal. May the Eternal, the Almighty, send a blessing on us and on all the Lord's people."

So it was when Israel departed from its slavery in Egypt, from its subjection to foreign rule, and entered into freedom. It was an exodus that determined everything else, the beginning of an irrevocable covenant between God and God's people. Later, in the clouds of Sinai, God made a solemn oath acknowledging that the people had been chosen and sent forth to freedom.

What, in this covenant, does Jesus still see before him?

When he breaks the bread and gives it to his disciples, he no longer believes that human community with God still exists. He is much closer to the prophet Jeremiah than to Moses. Jeremiah had seen Jerusalem going up in flames, its walls thrown down by the battering rams of the Babylonians, and he saw the people being led away to another miserable enslavement. Then Jeremiah wrote about a *new* covenant that God would make. The tables of the law written on stone were broken, but another time, at the end of the ages, God's word would be written on human hearts.

Jesus believes this in the hour of his Passover meal. Everything has to begin again, but altogether differently, so that human freedom may really come to pass. Had he ever in his life wished anything else than that people would stop talking about God "as it is written," outside themselves, on tablets or parchments, learning the words by heart and quoting them generation after generation, separating people into groups: the good and the bad, the insiders and the lost, those who are "finished," "perfected," and those who are to be finished off? When would God be interior to people, someone they can feel in their hearts, no longer a God of terror who has to impress people with lightning and thunder, but the voice of a sheer silence in the human heart, most powerful when most insignificant, most strongly felt and never greater than when one human being bows down before the greatness of another?

That was and is his whole concern, and that is why they wanted to kill him. Talking about freedom is one thing; living it is something else. Talking about God is simple, but really approaching God is a shattering experience with no security underfoot, and it is a confidence and comfort that needs no security. People always say they are free but when they meet someone who really is free they set up defenses against that person and try to protect themselves. All of us, more or less, think we are happy and content, but when we meet someone who really is happy and feels no need to protect himself or herself with hatred and struggle and competition, but is simply able to be selflessly good, we think we are seeing the devil in that person. We are all so "happy," and in hidden ways we are all suffering, and our inclination is to make others suffer, too.

How can light be brought into this darkness, and how can people be freed from these lies? It cannot be true that we have to keep taking innocent creatures and slaughtering them, smearing our doorposts with their blood, so that some kind of greedy demons will finally stop torturing human beings. This archaic, bloodthirsty, and grim ritual has been celebrated often enough. We do not need a Passover meal or a sacrificial holocaust anymore. What we need is, finally, to be serious about our real choices: humanity or death, hatred or love, terror or freedom. We need to put our talk to the test. Therefore there is no way out of the upper room, where that Passover was celebrated, that does not lead to the Mount of Olives and to Golgotha. Everything Jesus did and said was enough, but there remained the suspicion that if they just turned the screws a little tighter, they could get some different words out of him and force him to act differently. But what would that have proved? That it is possible to tear human beings into pieces as if they were loaves of bread; nothing more. And just as with the loaf, we will see that people have to have a reason for living. But the mystery of human beings is that they do not want to live just to keep themselves alive; they have to know why they are living. They need God as much as they need every crumb of bread. That is what is at stake.

The Church says that Jesus, in this hour in the upper room, instituted the sacrament of the priesthood and commanded his disciples to celebrate the meal of memorial and promise of the future reign of God with people in every age. If that is what it means to be priests, then we should all be priests: people who have power through their strength to bless others, to open heaven over every individual, and to show each one what it is to which he or she is called. Even the sacrament of the Eucharist has been used to create fear in whole generations of people. They were told they must be worthy if they were not to eat and drink judgment to themselves at the altar. What Jesus wanted was just the opposite: People should rest in God with such trust that they feel they are accepted without qualification or precondition, no matter what they have done. That is what Jesus stood for. No one can expect the hundredth sheep to find its own way back, but it is more important to God than the other ninety-nine. The God in whom Jesus believed was so important to him that he left heaven to be with human beings, to seek the lost and heal the sick. Jesus had the words of the prophet Ezekiel about the shepherds of the people on his lips: "You did not strengthen the weak nor heal the sick nor bind up the injured. You did not bring back the strayed nor seek the lost, but you lorded it over them harshly and brutally." If Jesus appointed priests at the hour of the Last Supper, they were to be shepherds, unlike the high priests of his own day, who had decided to kill the one who brings life.

Whenever, since that night, we celebrate a meal together, it should be done according to the mind of Jesus: that no guilt remains un-forgiven, that no separation between us is final, and that the division that parts us from God, from our own selves, and from other people is taken away. It should be a meal that anticipates the reign of God, a community of all people that shows that God is mightier than all fear and greater than all might. For nothing is stronger than love.

✝ Good Friday

22. It Is Finished

Standing by the cross of Jesus were his mother and his mother's
sister, Mary the wife of Clopas, and Mary of Magdala. When
Jesus saw his mother and the disciple there whom he loved, he
said to his mother, "Woman, behold, your son." Then he said to
the disciple, "Behold, your mother." And from that hour the
disciple took her into his home. After this, aware that everything
was now finished, in order that the scripture might be fulfilled,
Jesus said, "I thirst." There was a vessel filled with common
wine. So they put a sponge soaked in wine on a sprig of hyssop
and put it up to his mouth. When Jesus had taken the wine, he
said, "It is finished." And bowing his head, he handed over the
spirit (Jn 19:25-30).

With these words, the fourth Gospel concludes its account of
Christ's suffering. If we were to paint the scene as John imagines it,
we could not do as did the Gothic painters like Matthias Grünewald: a
Christ whose face and figure are rent by pain, a portrait of shame,
distress, and anguish. Instead, if we recreate the scene as John thinks
it should be, it might be like a Romanesque crucifix: a king entering

into his glory. He overcomes the challenge of death, fear, and the abyss. Here we behold the glory of God and the glory of the Son of Humanity.

From the point of view of the other evangelists, we could ask John how he came to see things this way. We would have to join Matthew's gospel in asking, "Don't you know, John, that in the hour of Golgotha the sun was darkened and the earth quaked? How can you speak of glory and exaltation on the cross?" Would it not be closer to the truth if we painted the scene on the hill of Calvary somewhat as did Hieronymus Bosch at the beginning of the sixteenth century? Here we see Jesus on the road to the "place of the skull," surrounded by a group of people whose physiognomy and attitude reveal how incapable they are of understanding anything at all of Jesus' intention and his concerns. Their eyes are bulging with greed and stupidity, their mouths screaming; they are grasping, mean, envious, so contorted as to be positively disgusting. In fact, to say that these faces are bestial would be an insult to the beasts. But these are human beings. Among them stands Christ, his eyes weary with exhaustion and sorrow. They ask us, as beholders, to consider in which of the countenances around him we find ourselves reflected or hope never to see ourselves again.

But John would have insisted that his Romanesque picture of Jesus' crucifixion is a correct one, as contrasted with images of Jesus' despair in God and human beings. He would tell us: When you read how Christ died, do not regard his death as different from his life. Everything he embodied is like the answer to a prayer that is gradually brought to its perfection. When you hear how the soldiers rattled their dice cups to gamble for the garment that covered his nakedness, do not look merely at the external cynicism, the brutality of their materialism, the infamy of their coarseness. Open your Bible to the psalm that begins with a desperate cry, Psalm 22: "My God, my God, why have you forsaken me?" It ends with a description of the beginning of God's rule over human beings, and in between there is this scene: "For my vesture they cast lots." And when you hear how Jesus cries out in his thirst, read the lament of the sufferer in Psalm 22: "My tongue cleaves to my jaws; to the dust of death you have brought me down. . . . I can count all my bones." No, John was not deluding himself when he described this scene. The purpose of his picturing it this way is to drive the severity of the contradiction to the utmost, to the point where we, in the abyss of despair, meet God.

So we should not paint this scene on Golgotha like a Romanesque crucifix, lifting the royal figure on the cross against a gleaming golden background. That is not what John meant, but rather the reverse: The whole world is darkness, the background is entirely black, but if you want to see an escape route in this world, if you want to find light in the midst of darkness, then look at the figure of the Crucified. For "the light shines in the darkness," but the world loved darkness more than light. Thus begins the fourth Gospel, and everything that will be said in the passion narrative seems to be a proof of that paradox.

No matter the names of the actors in this execution scene; there is some of each of them in all of us.

There are the calculating people, the Judas types. How much is a human being worth? How much can you get for one? Don't say, "Well, it used to be that human beings were sold in the southern United States, in market stalls between the tobacco and the bananas, for twenty or thirty dollars apiece—but that was 130 years ago!" If you look carefully you will see what kind of power Judas still has. How deviously human relationships are organized by calculation: counting, accounting, adding and subtracting, weighing and balancing! What do I get from that person? How much can I get out of him or her? What kind of profit can I make from them by calculating, manipulating, valuing? How much is it worth to have a relationship with another human being? And the betraying and killing goes on.

There are people like Peter, the pragmatic types. They insist that one should know what to do in every situation. They have the scepter or the sword in their hands. They also have a lot of big words to say, and they are "man enough" to intervene. Their world is so simple: You have to do this or that, you have to act, you have to establish standards, set things right, even things out. These Peter-types wound others, and they don't solve a single problem, but they are immensely clever in their narrow-mindedness, diligent, and in a certain sense even courageous. They appear whenever possible as the saviors of humanity and of all that is holy.

Then there are people in the mold of Annas and Caiaphas, diplomatic types, the logicians of history. They know precisely according to which laws people may be measured in the political scale or in that of canon law or public rationality. It is always better for the individual to die in order to prevent greater damage. They are ever responsible, wise, and armed with good arguments, but their hearts are frozen, their feelings are cold, and they only have to open their mouths to utter death sentences. Annas and Caiaphas are always acting in the service of responsibility, order, and reason, but everything they do increases inhumanity, corruption, and the enormous sum of deaths. There are people like Pilate, who administer power. They are the functionaries, the bureaucrats of the system, themselves powerless and always anxious. They manage in the end to sit on the throne without guilt. "I don't know why Jesus should be executed," they say, but the conclusion they draw is, "Take him, then, and do whatever you want." It is remarkable how the responsibilities are shared, how the law is misused to create suffering, and the process is made all the easier if one does not believe there is such a thing as truth. What an advantage it is if there is nothing solid in human life, nothing for which one could risk one's heart or one's life. If you believe nothing, you can do anything. There is nothing lasting, and so you can overcome everything by being soft as a jellyfish. You don't need character or conviction or reflection; it is all a business, a contrivance, part of the power game. Anyone who has understood all this can hold court on the stone pavement, surrounded, of course, by other representatives of legitimacy. One is careful of days and hours, one knows exactly what zones can be entered on the day of Passover and which cannot. They all have the word of God on their lips, and they all have their sacred laws, their ordinances, their regulations, and their rules.

We only have to go on reading and we can see, step by step and line by line, that in the passion story we encounter no world but our own. None of it is historically unique or accidental. This is the way it always is. There will always be the calculating types, the pragmatic people, the logicians, the cynics, the representatives of order, the bureaucrats, and their game is our life, or rather our death. In the end come the myrmidons, the people who execute the orders, those who have finally quashed their thinking under steel helmets and whose bodies have become instruments for killing. They will keep themselves clear of any hurt by their meanness, mockery, contempt, and lack of understanding. If anyone asks them why, they will click their heels and say, "We are acting on orders."

The question is, what can we believe in when we are faced with a life that no longer deserves the consideration we show for it? There was a group of women under the cross, and two men waiting for the body of the dead man: Joseph of Arimathea and that Nicodemus who had heard in his midnight conversation with Jesus that there is such a thing as the miracle of rebirth and the freedom and almighty power of the Spirit that blows where it will. There was the trust of a man who offered his own tomb because he did not believe in the power of graves. And there was the magnificent woman from the fishing village of Magdala who had been freed from seven evil spirits and who remained faithful to Jesus because he had taught her how to recover her own self and her own ideas.

What do we believe in? That is the question. If we see only the external appearance of Golgotha, the world will go on as it is, and those of us who are in it will be so discouraged that we will have to go with it.

But if we look deeper, if we look in faith at the meaning of Golgotha, we will see that after this it will no longer be possible for human beings or circumstances to create *that* fear that causes people to deny themselves and all that they love. After this there is a space for sensitive feelings in which nothing is decided by the sword, but instead by the power of listening, understanding, slowly ripening patience, and kindness, where there is no further need for justifications, but a way of seeing the need and fear even in those who make themselves so great, who seem so strong and perhaps are most vulnerable to themselves and to circumstances. But the almighty power of circumstances will no longer exist, there will be an end to the selling of people according to a superior logic when we have understood how magnificent every single person is in himself or herself. Serving people is more important than higher, derived purposes that are more and more removed from genuine humanity. Bowing before the majesty of the human being next to us teaches us to love, and love can never die. Therefore becoming a witness to the death of Jesus is a slow process of comprehending an indestructible glory. What are we afraid of, for God's sake? What are we afraid of? We are worried about our damned good reputations and our lousy few decades of life on this earth, our integrity and our health and the fatness of our purses. But are those really things worth worrying about? Do they represent genuine values if we can discover what power rests in the enchantment of love, what fantasy in our own hearts, what courage and strength in our heads? Who is there around us then who can say or decide anything for us? The Pilate-types are fearful, the Annas and Caiaphas boys are corrupt, the self-declared companions like Peter are untrustworthy and unable to fend off the people like

Judas. But they cannot deny all that life offers: union in love, friendship, and the universal sisterhood and brotherhood of the reign of God! Faith is stronger than the evidence of the senses, and the cross is not a cross, but the beginning of life, a life worthy of the name and a life that can either begin this afternoon or, quite literally, never.

The Easter Vigil

23. Fire from Stones

Readings: Gen 1:1-2:2; Ex 14:10-15:1; Ezek 37:1-14

The Easter Vigil celebration is not really the proclamation of Jesus' resurrection, but rather an ascending preparation for beholding the empty tomb. Resurrection is the mystery at the heart of our lives, but it is inexpressibly difficult to state it in words. "We must be silent about the things we cannot say," in the words of the famous philosopher Ludwig Wittgenstein, but he himself says just before this, "The mystical is something inexpressible." In this Easter night we enter the realm of mystical experience, and because the words are difficult to find, the Church presents us in these night hours with a wealth of images drawn from the treasures of all the ages of human religion. If we pass in review the series of images that we evoke in this celebration, we encounter the oldest feelings of humanity, before time, drawn from the riches of their longing and hope in the midst of a world so often ruined and threatening. What can we expect?

One of the earliest experiences of humanity must have been the thing that we introduce, quite routinely, at the beginning of the Easter Vigil celebration: sacred fire. We can estimate that this element that causes animals to flee in terror must have been placed in human hands more than three hundred thousand years ago. It was the first real and radical step by which we left the realm of animals and became human, a dangerous step, which is why the earliest popular myths speak of a successful theft on the part of human beings, by which they acquired something that was the property of the gods. But what really happened? People must have discovered that they could make fire from the least fiery of materials, from dead stones struck together. So the Church's ritual even today prescribes that the spark of the Easter fire must be drawn from stone, and we rob it of almost all its meaning when we reduce it to the flick of a lighter.

Such images reflect something about our own hearts and the way we often feel: so weary that our heaviness weighs us down to the ground, each of us bearing the mortgage of a history that seems to involve thousands of years, in which everything has slowly frozen until it lies the prey of the wind and rain, gradually becoming smaller and weaker. Whole epochs of our lives can seem that way, but now the experience that in this Easter night the Church evokes for us in the person of Christ should be that a living spark can spring from what is dead, and from that spark can emerge a completely different element of light and warmth to take possession of us. When we begin to seem to ourselves like freezing animals in the midnight of our lives, this image of the fire from the stone is the one thing that keeps us alive. The people who first discovered it did not know what they were doing and had no words with which to explain it. Fallen twigs and dead wood have long since lost their green freshness, and yet if we rub them together, patiently and stubbornly, and blow living breath on them, we can draw fire from this dead stuff and kindle it into warmth and light. If that is so, then can there be anything in this world that we can say is really and finally dead?

There must have been a first time when human beings opened the dark walls of this world and something like a beam from another world fell into the night of life, something we do not see but from that time have begun to intuit. With that tiny intuition we have made our way through the darkness of the world as human beings, which is what we are, and since then we have not been willing to believe that death has the last word over our existence. In reality it is the testimony of love, which has such power in our hearts that it brings light to our eyes and warms our souls. Love refuses to believe that anything that is born can simply wither and freeze and be past and gone as if it never had been.

The human beings must have invited the whole spectrum of nature to the fire, so that it could be filled with poetic love songs to the immortality of all that is, especially human life.

In the evening sky above us we can still see the winter stars of Orion, just about to sink in the west. In a few weeks it will be withdrawn from our eyes and the summer constellations will shine forth from the darkness of the night. Can it also be that the things we can never reach, the stars set in heaven, will also disappear and, after a fixed interval, rise again? Is not everything a great rhythm of going *and* coming? The moon waxes and wanes in the course of a month. All creation in the northern hemisphere shares in the rhythm of the year, in summer and winter, in fading and blooming, in disappearing and reappearing, and all of it shapes itself into a song of the immortality of life, which knows death only for the sake of renewal. Nothing really vanishes forever. It is astonishing that when we stand at the grave of a person we deeply love, we still renew and continue something that people very different from us began more than seven thousand years ago. We put flowers on the grave that receives the mortal husk of our fellow human being, and by this gesture we try to say that, even if we are only a part of nature, every flower carries with it a message of life. What goes away will come again, and death is only a transition. In the Persian caves, early people left traces of flowers for their dead, and we celebrate Easter on the first Sunday after the first full moon of spring, when life is renewed in the heavens and on the earth. This is the great song of a creation that is marvelous in its changes and in the rhythm in which it was formed.

It is therefore right, in a very basic sense, that we should hear the texts of the Easter Vigil from the lips of women. It is they who are called to speak of the resurrection. The passion story we heard on Good Friday is only about the works and deeds of men, and it is a gruesome and bloody story. But from of old it is women who are the protectors of life. They had to watch the fire when the men went out to the hunt or to war. They warmed it in their hands and sheltered it against the wind. In their maturing, they embodied the earth itself, and in the periodic monthly rhythms of their own bodies they imaged the mystery of the moon. Theirs from of old is the power to create life, and no one could solve the mystery of its beginning. Women are called to read the message of the resurrection, for in their whole essence they are closer to it than men. "Why does anything exist?" is the question of the first reading for this celebration. Only we humans can question everything around us; for us, nothing is self-explanatory. Now we know that life must have been formed out of the apparent chaos of our solar system and our planet, in a series of stages lasting more than five million years and according to laws that are wise and good and that, at last, brought us into being as well. At no point, not even at the end of one of the days of creation, is it possible to say what the next day will bring, or what will be the next step in the development of life. Every point in this great progress of creation is mysterious, inexplicable in its details, and full of creative fantasy—in short, the whole is divine. But when are we in a position to see the creation as a song of praise and to find in its every detail the work of God that is its source? Resurrection is this, too: being thankful for the unearned gift of our existence, together with all the beauty of the world.

There are two experiences that hinder us in this, and they are the subjects of the next two readings. First is imprisonment and the fear of other people, as experienced by Israel in the land of Egypt. Does it not often happen that we see our life being driven by the need to satisfy strange compulsions, so that we are powerless to determine our own actions or even to formulate a single thought or wish of our own, much less carry it out? And yet this reading about the exodus of Israel from Egypt—this text of the Passover night that applies to this evening's celebration—also tells us that there is much more in us than "you should," and "you must," more than being handed over to the violence of foreign rulers. There is also in us a great longing for freedom, and no matter how much it may be suppressed, it remains stronger than the fetters imposed from outside. A whole nation like Israel is able to put itself in motion—mainly fleeing in fear, it is true, but still following the way it must go, even into the desert when that is the way of freedom. Everyone who tries it will have an experience like that of Israel on the shore of the Red Sea. We have scarcely taken the first steps on the way to freedom when our former masters appear as our pursuers, chasing us with chariots that are faster than our running feet, and very soon we will find barriers before us that we do not dare to cross because we have never put our feet in such a place before. Everything looks bottomless, endless, and insecure. The miracle on the road to freedom that deserves to be called an image of resurrection is that Israel goes forward through the water of death and dares to reach the other shore, and there is no human dependency or human fear for them any more, because nothing matters but God's call, which again is like fire from stone, sparks from dust, a light in the darkness and warmth in cold times, a beginning beyond death, a new spring of life.

The prophet Ezekiel tells us that there is something even worse than external enslavement, and that is to feel completely dry and deserted in ourselves. It may seize the chosen people themselves one day, as if, far from their real calling, they brought others nothing but misery and confusion, sin and wickedness. Can't it happen that one day we begin to get on our own nerves so much that we hate ourselves for what we are and no longer trust ourselves to do what is right, even to the point that the most important of our experiences begin to tell us that we have done everything wrong and have even done harm to the people who have tried to accompany us on our way? This is a dreadful vision, perhaps the worst of all, harder even than our destiny to physical death. But that is not all there is, says Ezekiel, thinking of Israel; even in the midst of guilt and chaos, there is a new beginning and a new commitment and the miracle of insight, of rising courage and regeneration. In the hands of God, nothing is finally lost. This, too, is resurrection.

What does all this mean: the witness of nature, the testimony of history, the words of our hearts? The Church tells us at a certain point in the Easter Vigil that it is like the return of the bells and like a new song. We can make the fire so hot that it melts the dead stone and metal pours out. When it cools, it can be shaped into a bell. Our hearts could be the same. Wherever they are struck, they swing into a pure, harmonic sound, and all the conflicts are resolved in a single music of joy beyond all chaos, beyond the grave, beyond the night. That is what this night festival wants to tell us: We are going to the light, we are on the way to see the empty tombs.

Easter Sunday

24. Love and Death

After the sabbath, as the first day of the week was dawning, Mary Magdalene and the other Mary came to see the tomb. And behold, there was a great earthquake; for an angel of the Lord descended from heaven, approached, rolled back the stone, and sat upon it. His appearance was like lightning and his clothing was white as snow. The guards were shaken with fear of him and became like dead men. Then the angel said to the women in reply, "Do not be afraid! I know that you are seeking Jesus the crucified. He is not here, for he has been raised just as he said. Come and see the place where he lay. Then go quickly and tell his disciples, 'He has been raised from the dead, and he is going before you to Galilee; there you will see him.' Behold, I have told you." Then they went away quickly from the tomb, fearful yet overjoyed, and ran to announce this to his disciples. And behold, Jesus met them on their way and greeted them. They approached, embraced his feet, and did him homage. Then Jesus said to them, "Do not be afraid. Go tell my brothers to go to Galilee, and there they will see me."

> *While they were going, some of the guard went into the city and told the chief priests all that had happened. They assembled with the elders and took counsel; then they gave a large sum of money to the soldiers, telling them, "You are to say, 'His disciples came by night and stole him while we were asleep.' And if this gets to the ears of the governor, we will satisfy [him] and keep you out of trouble." The soldiers took the money and did as they were instructed. And this story has circulated among the Jews to the present [day] (Mt 28:1-15).*

There are only two essential subjects in human life, love and death, and there is no fear greater than that of the dawning Easter morning, the fear that death has the power to conquer love. Death works so grimly that in the normal course of nature it tears asunder people who love each other so much they can scarcely imagine being separated. It can happen without warning, abrupt and sudden as an attack.

When the Lord died, the earth quaked and the sun was darkened. So says the Christian legend, and it is the truth. When a person we are so close to is torn from us, we feel the earth sway under our feet, and we see all the light of the world snuffed out. But the grim truth is that nature has no interest either in our happiness or in our pain. The earth goes on turning, and the sun rises and sets, indifferent to our fate. Then aren't the cynics right when they say that it does not pay to take love so seriously? Isn't it really foolishness to believe what love teaches us and to think that individual human beings who, love tells us, are infinitely precious, are also infinitely great, beautiful, and gifted with eternal life?

Even worse than natural death is the dying we human beings can impose on ourselves through our deadly practice of anxiety and cynicism that does not and *will* not see anything but death. This is what tortured the women most as they went to the tomb: that the logic of violence and destruction seemed to be validated, as if in this world goodness, understanding, humanity, and freedom were nothing but dead words, and as if now and forever only the heavy boots of the mighty were the stronger force, and as if the most revolting despisers of life were apparently upheld. It is so simple to kill and get rid of something precious, and what is left for any human being when the one to whom his or her heart belongs is taken away?

When the Egyptians anointed the body of a dead person, they did so in the belief that the dead live on in the tomb, and they gave the person all the food and other things required to supply his or her needs in the chambers of eternity. The women who went to the Lord's tomb could not believe that. They knew that the body decays and that no power of nature could change that. But they thought, contrary to all cynicism, that love implies fidelity.

Joseph of Arimathea thought the same way when he offered his own tomb for the crucified Jesus. It is possible to besmirch what is precious, but there is also a duty of decency, an inner attachment in fidelity. In the face of the barbarity that had been practiced, it was already a great deal to do even that, and thereby to erect at least a narrow bridge between Good Friday and Easter. But what kind of life is it that feels itself more obligated to the dead than to the living? How can we live, when every road on earth leads to a grave? We cling to the monuments and the mortal remains, but that is no way to live.

It is a great thing that the women went to the tomb on that Easter morning. How different would the story of the Lord's passion have been, if anyone had ever put any faith in their word! There was the warning of Pilate's wife, who in the night before the execution saw what our life would be like after her husband said those words at the stone pavement: "What difference does it make to me?" and "I wash my hands in innocence," and "Look to it yourselves." Our lives would become a nightmare, that she knew, and she told him so in the crucial moment, but he did not listen. The woman who spoke to Peter by the charcoal fire said to his face, "You are one of those from Galilee," trying to force him into an honest, courageous, and public admission. It got her nowhere.

The realists in this world, even the male disciples without exception, fled for their lives from the violence and destruction of life; they got away to Galilee, but they fled to a life that is no life at all.

Only a few women remained under the cross, because they had no other choice. Mary, the woman from Magdala, had seven evil spirits beset and pursue her before she met the Lord. Only then did her life take on a human shape as she regained her inner coherence, her true self. It scarcely seems to matter to the realists of this world whether someone's life is split into three, or five, or seven evil spirits: prescribed roles, compulsions, excuses, obligations, petty meannesses. You have to be very sensitive to think this world is crazy and go crazy over it, to know that Jesus the dreamer was much more right than all the others. The women who went to the grave on Easter morning did so with the feeling that this dead man was more alive than all of them—the executioners, the murderers, the survivors throughout the land. But they could not live that way. The tomb is a nowhere land, the home of homelessness.

In this moment of their bitterest despair, the angel of God descends from heaven and takes pity on human misery by revealing a reality that exists all the time, but that we, with our tearful eyes and our despairing hearts, cannot see. It is an image of God that we carry in us and hear in our souls. With the eyes of our spirit, we can see the angel who wrests the stone from the grave and sits victorious upon it.

It will always happen that people will try to imprison other human beings, even put guards before their tombs and forbid any disturbance of the quiet within which life is stirring, to put a stop to any interference in the routines of non-life. These guardian spirits are now, for the first time, afraid. *They* are like the dead when life breaks out, and it is suddenly clear that from this time forever it will be impossible to imprison a human reality in any kind of tomb. People will not be able to do it, and nature certainly not, because God who created us desires that we should live; otherwise we would not exist. It took all of eternity to produce something as precious as each individual one of us. We will be able to live for all eternity. On this morning that truth is clear in the hearts of two women who behold the face of God, which is powerful enough to wake the dead.

It is terrible to seek the Beloved as the Crucified One, apparently defeated, shamed, destroyed, but we no longer need to seek life in the abode of the dead. We no longer need to feel that our love has been defeated by the course of events. Externally, they may be what they will be. This event will not be written down in Pilate's scribal records. It will not even enter the annals of humanity outside the New Testament. It will not be recorded as such in the history books. But it is powerful enough to change our hearts forever. In the future we can approach one another, no longer with a message of despair, but turning from the tomb and toward others, those we want to see as Jesus' disciples see, and say to them, "You need no longer believe in fear or in the power of the means used to bring people to their knees. You, too, can believe in life." If we take the road this way, in each other's company, this Gospel tells us that the Lord will come to meet us—the one we love, the one we know to be the foundation of everything that makes this life worth living—and we will fall at his feet and kiss them, worshiping him.

In all the other appearance narratives the first word is, "Do not be afraid!" because the figure from another world, from the divine realm, is so overpowering in its appearance. Here the first word of the Risen One to the women is a joyful greeting: *"Chairete!*—Hail!" Only then, from a quite different point of view, does he add, "Do not be afraid!" We must never again fear the one who causes us to live, and neither shall we fear the world around us. We will no longer need to fear anyone or anything for the sake of our threatened and endangered lives. Our life is secure, even in the face of death. The Song of Songs says that love is as strong as death, but we can affirm since that first Easter morning, irrevocably, that love is infinitely stronger than death. This earthly existence we lead is only an appearance, a first phase of reality, nothing final, but the beginning of eternity, the opening of eyes that will see forever. We are already on our way to Galilee together. Jesus himself is no longer talking about his disciples at this moment, but about us as his sisters and brothers, as if everything he wanted to say was already reality. All of us together are like sisters and brothers, and there is now only *one* power of love.

\\Whenever we encounter a human being in such a way that we feel absolutely certain of the infinity of that person's worth and the eternity of his or her life, that is Easter. No power in the world will ever again be able to remove love from our hearts. Our body will pass away, but our soul, our immortal essence, will lift itself to the light of the stars like a golden bird returning to its home. "Behold," says the angel at the tomb, "I have told you."

25. Is the Tomb Empty?

When the sabbath was over, Mary Magdalene, Mary, the mother of James, and Salome bought spices so that they might go and anoint him. Very early when the sun had risen, on the first day of the week, they came to the tomb. They were saying to one another, "Who will roll back the stone for us from the entrance to the tomb?" When they looked up, they saw that the stone had been rolled back; it was very large. On entering the tomb they saw a young man sitting on the right side, clothed in a white robe, and they were utterly amazed. He said to them, "Do not be amazed! You seek Jesus of Nazareth, the crucified. He has been raised; he is not here. Behold the place where they laid him. But go and tell his disciples and Peter, 'He is going before you to Galilee; there you will see him, as he told you.'" Then they went out and fled from the tomb, seized with trembling and bewilderment. They said nothing to anyone, for they were afraid (Mk 16:1-8).

"But you, my dear sisters and brothers, say to the disciples: 'He is going before you to Galilee.'" With these words, the Gospel of Mark ends, and that is the end of everything there is to say about the story of Jesus and the history of humanity, for we have acquired an eternally valid insight: The grave has no power over life.

From the earliest days of humanity, there has been a question sweeping through human history, gently at first, later like a stormy wind. The more human consciousness has developed, the more clearly has death appeared as a problem. The more we humans have grown to the point of discovering our individuality, the more lost we feel in the processes of nature, and for the first time on this earth, our human spirit formulates questions to which the whole world can offer us no answer. From the beginnings of humanity, therefore, we have called on our senses to give testimony against themselves. The walls of the world's prison have become thinner and thinner under pressure from the growing human spirit.

In the early days of humanity, the miracle of light must have brought astonishment as a testimony to the soul as the light of the moon re-emerged from the three days of its death and the morning sun arose from its nightly dying. What the Church gathers from the store of human memory to celebrate the vigil of Easter is like a collection of experiences and recollections from a time before memory: the miracle of fire, the miracle of renewal. It is possible to breathe upon and rub dry, dead wood, from which the life has fled, in such a way that light, warmth, and beauty spring from it. It is possible to strike hard stones against one another in such a way that sparks of light spring from them.

It is possible for the wind to blow over the water in such a way that life emerges on the land. It is possible, even in the dryness of the desert and the cold of the winter, for grain to grow from the earth and flowers from the frozen ground. Then is it impossible that the soul should arise from the grave and that eternal life should spring from the dead body?

It is deeply moving to behold how, in tens of thousands of years of human experience, the conviction of the indestructibility of life has emerged like a slowly growing hymn. No other message can really enable us to sustain even our few decades of earthly existence. What would we be, then, without our confidence in eternity? We would cling to the earth with our bodies until there would be no more difference between flesh and dust, and we would use the best efforts of our minds to protect ourselves from the approach of death. But in its fear, our alert reason would repeatedly beat life into weapons of death, and in our attempts to secure our life, we would never really begin to live. Burdened by despair, shadowed by hopelessness, tortured by cares, and infiltrated by inhumanity, we would not exist, but vegetate, more aware of our fate than the animals that suffer death but do not experience it.

We know how threatened our existence is. Only we human beings, in the alertness of our minds, can be forever and irrevocably individual. We alone know that, in the circling of the spheres and the course of nature, we will exist only once. What kind of response is given us against the power of death to quench us? Only one: that even beyond the world there is God, the world's Creator, an absolute will, an endless love to which we owe our existence; and we are not thrown into existence as a blind sowing and a result of laws and accidents. There is a will that desires us to be, and there is a love that desires us to live. The course run by humanity as a whole is the same as that destined for every individual. A genuine person is formed only in relationship to another person who is absolutely devoted to us and who will not let us go until the rind and the husk fall away. Such people are like the Jesus whom the disciples knew and whom the women on Easter morning sought again, beyond his death. There are people who enter our lives like an awakening out of a long sleep, like a call from death to happiness, like being torn out of bitter dreams and opening our eyes to the light. There are people who enter our lives and bring about a transformation of everything, so that growing older is like being reborn and like a new beginning, so that the vanishing of the years shapes itself into ripening rings of happiness, contentment, and the beginning of joy, and the old fetters, the prescriptions of fear, the constrictions of environment, the roles prescribed by others, all cease to have any meaning. Jesus must have entered the lives of these women with that kind of force. They left their marriages, their families, their previous callings; they gave up their incomes, broke every tie, laid themselves open to public shame; but they knew that they were indestructibly wed.

Mary, the woman from Magdala, can represent all those whose lives have been shredded and devoured by seven evil spirits until they are no longer recognizable. If someone asks us who we are, one spirit after another will talk and talk—who we were as children, as teenagers, as young adults, as grown-ups—and we always had to exist but dared not live, we were always steered through life and had no chance to develop a real self. But here is the truth of an indestructible beginning, the initial moment of an eternal happiness. In that power, life begins to open out for us like a road, and it is as when sparks are born from stone, and grain from the earth, and fire from the dust. Enthusiasm, passion, joy, fantasy begin to consume our lives like torches. Suddenly the endlessness of our lives does not seem to enclose us like a trap or a prison. Suddenly the confidence that these few decades of life are a beginning of eternity begins to grow. What does the tomb then have to say to us? Dust and the earth may encompass the dead bodies, and the sarcophagus may wrap the firmament with all its stars like a linen shroud, but our real life, beginning and ripening in love, will be indestructible. In the short space of our earthly existence we can gather all the hours of happiness when the clocks stand still and time is concentrated to a single point that must endure forever. Even now we can gather the fantasies born of our dreams and longings, the hints of life as eternal and indestructible, when only the truth of the soul, the purity of the word, and the infinite power of love are valid. That is the goal toward which we can live.

Was the tomb empty on Easter morning? If we ask the historians, they will discuss the question till it comes out our ears, but the image is true for all time: Tombs are no longer tombs, but bridges to eternity. They are places in which to begin a dialogue with eternal life. Our life is a pilgrimage backward to everything Jesus taught us in the villages of Galilee and the town on Lake Gennesaret. He will always be going before us with his message of humanity and of the indestructibility of each of us. His way of living according to the words of the Sermon on the Mount provoked all kinds of resistance and formed the basis for his execution on the cross, but his resurrection is the beginning of the certainty that in the future, life will only be worth living in his freedom, his generosity of heart, his universal love. For each of us is born for the light, a child of the stars, a daughter or son of the eternal God, and together we are on the pilgrim way in the power of love, back to Galilee, to the Mount of Transfiguration, to the place where heaven touches earth. We will live forever, and the power of fear, the power of despair, the shadow of guilt will disappear as in a dream. The day began on the first Sabbath morning, early, as the sun was rising and the stone was rolled away from the grave of our hearts.

26. *Whom Do You Seek?*

On the first day of the week, Mary of Magdala came to the tomb early in the morning, while it was still dark, and saw the stone removed from the tomb. So she ran and went to Simon Peter and to the other disciple whom Jesus loved, and told them, "They have taken the Lord from the tomb, and we don't know where they put him." So Peter and the other disciple went out and came to the tomb. They both ran, but the other disciple ran faster than Peter and arrived at the tomb first; he bent down and saw the burial cloths there, and the cloth that had covered his head, not with the burial cloths but rolled up in a separate place. Then the other disciple also went in, the one who had arrived at the tomb first, and he saw and believed. For they did not yet understand the scripture that he had to rise from the dead. Then the disciples returned home.

But Mary stayed outside the tomb weeping. And as she wept, she bent over into the tomb and saw two angels in white sitting there, one at the head and one at the feet where the body of Jesus had been. And they said to her, "Woman, why are you weeping?" She said to them, "They have taken my Lord, and I don't know where they laid him." When she had said this, she turned around and saw Jesus there, but did not know it was Jesus. Jesus said to her, "Woman, why are you weeping? Whom are you looking

*for?" She thought it was the gardener and said to him, "Sir, if
you carried him away, tell me where you laid him, and I will take
him." Jesus said to her, "Mary!" She turned and said to him in
Hebrew, "Rabbouni," which means Teacher. Jesus said to her,
"Stop holding on to me, for I have not yet ascended to the Father.
But go to my brothers and tell them, 'I am going to my Father
and your Father, to my God and your God.'" Mary of Magdala
went and announced to the disciples, "I have seen the Lord,"
and what he told her (Jn 20:1-18).*

What kind of experience is represented by the symbolic expression,
resurrection of the dead?

The Gospel for Easter morning, in the story of the women going to
the tomb, describes resurrection in terms of the ability to see graves
opened and life standing in the place of death. It is an old experience,
so deeply rooted in us human beings that probably our own consciousness, our own humanity would never have been able to mature and
assert itself unless we had also developed the ability to see the world
in some other way besides the vision of our physical eyes. If we see
ourselves only as children of this world, we are lost, and the more we
awaken to our own individuality, to knowledge of the beauty and the
vulnerable greatness of our individual existence, the more do we
despair at being able to exist only for the few years we are on earth. If
the last word on our existence were to be that we are only what we see,
something hastily assembled and surrounded by shadows, the few
years that we are here would be nothing but a fleeting dream, something unreal and incomprehensible, almost nothing but a passing mood
and a game played by nature.

For that reason, symbolic literature on human life begins very early
and extends as far into the past as we can gather evidence from human
history. The clearest, most extensive and many-faceted evidence of
belief in a life after death is found in Egyptian remains. Their language
found its way into Christian belief and remains the basis of many of
our symbols and rituals. This is the first powerful expression of
confidence that we human beings are really not composed of the dust
of the earth but are essentially sun creatures, so that the golden light of
the sun in the heavens breathes in us. The sun never dies in our lives,
or rather, it dies again every evening in order to convey that there is no
death; it is overcome by the power of light and warmth with which it

recalls everything to life each morning. We human beings are of that same nature, and death is unreal. Our earthly life is only a shadowy dream, a fleeting reflection of the genuine reality that is high above our heads. With every dawn, when the birds, animals, and opening flowers turn to the light with their songs and their beauty, our soul is invited to prayers of thanksgiving and trust. There is no death. There is only a gateway of night through which we pass; it opens the way to an imperishable world. All things are in the act of being transformed, and this process flows onward toward a world in which all is permanent. Christianity did not have to teach us that, because people had known it in their deepest thoughts thousands of years earlier. At any rate, that was what they hoped for increasingly, the more human they became. The ability to see graves as empty things or to understand them as filled with images of eternity is an art that is confirmed for us by the testimony of love: There can never be a final parting. Time passes, but the divine world, the sphere of the stars and the realm of the sun, remains forever and is always ready to receive us on the farther shore.

What the women expected and hoped for as they went to the tomb on Easter morning, and what we call resurrection, is something different, more intensely human, more existentially expansive. The earliest and latest formulae in the letters of Paul, and later in the speeches in the fourth Gospel, are the first passages that clearly interpret Jesus' resurrection as a transformation of our life here on earth. It is not that Jesus was the first to establish the belief in a continued life or further existence after death. He received this confidence from his ancestral inheritance, from large groups within Judaism who believed it, and he himself defended this conviction against the Sadducees. Much more important than confessing this hope as a piece of doctrine was what Jesus made of it. He *lived* his life against death, and he did not want us to begin to live that life only when we have physically departed from the earth. He saw with his own eyes that we human beings, in the midst of life, bury ourselves like cave dwellers in invisible graves covered with heavy stones, out of fear of the devastating fact that we must die. We set up defenses against it and in the end are more vulnerable to death. We make death a weapon by which we can assert ourselves and spread fear, and we live more and more as prisoners of the same fears. This phantom with which death destroys us—long before it arrives in the physical sense—is what Jesus wanted to remove. He wanted our confidence in God's faithfulness and nearness to be so immediate, to make it so real and unbroken, that there would disappear from our heads, our hearts, and our hands all the fearful imaginings, the defensive weapons, and the stirrings of hatred that we drag around with us as if that were perfectly normal.

The women who went to the tomb on Easter morning must have sensed how much power for genuine life went forth from Jesus. We know almost nothing of the woman from Magdala, except the brief note in the Gospel of Luke that she had been possessed by seven evil spirits. Let us take this woman who brings us the message of resurrection as representative of all of us threatened with the loss of everything, even our own personalities, subject to the extremes of alienation and abandonment, if it were not for the chance to find in the figure of Jesus a place where we are lifted up and restored to ourselves. So at the side of the man from Nazareth she must have rediscovered the words to express herself and to respond to the question, "Who are you?" with "I," with her own name, with words that make sense, with ideas derived from her own experience, so that the eternal tumult of lies, the brokenness of the masquerade, the whole articulation of internalized compulsions is swept away like a crowd of obsessions and demons. Jesus must have the kind of power that restores confidence in life, and thereby begins the resurrection of the dead even now.

That power is so enormous that the fourth Gospel is in a certain sense quite historically correct when it puts words in Jesus' mouth like those spoken to Martha at the raising of Lazarus. "Do you believe in the resurrection?" he asks the weeping woman. And she says, "I believe in the resurrection at the last day." The Egyptians could also have said that, but Jesus' response expresses what is uniquely Christian in our belief: "I *am* the resurrection and the life. Those who believe in me will not taste death any more, even though they die." Nothing is in the distant future; *today* it is possible to begin to live, even if it is a life like that of the young men in the fiery furnace. The force of fear and the flames of death no longer have the power to burn and destroy.

Then we must add what Good Friday had to mean for this group of women, the only ones who remained under the cross: that it is possible to destroy even and especially the one who so courageously said, "Those who believe in me will not taste death any more, even though they die." It would be anarchy, it would be dangerous, it would be the end of the iron-clad order of things if our life were as free as that and if we were able to love so straightforwardly and simply strike off our fetters, breaking through the dungeons of the fear of death. There *must* be something that can be done to stop it. There *is* something to be done. Our body can be destroyed, and our lips can go on speaking only as long as we can move them, and the articulation of our thoughts is dependent on the activity of our cerebral cortex. If the body is destroyed, the spirit itself may be eliminated in its earthly dimension. Good Friday represented the attempt to stamp out this incipient life as quickly as possible, so that it might not spread and become an epidemic of danger to good order, institutions, tyranny, and everything that kills and is falsely dubbed "a secure life." They did it. It was quite simple: All you have to do is twist the law a little, twist the human body a little—the soul can be tortured out of it very easily. But what does it prove? For these women who stuck it out on Good Friday, everything died in that hour on Golgotha. Only for those for whom everything dies with Jesus—because he means everything to them—is there an end to the death that has power over life. If things go on after that, the world goes on turning, but nothing "normal" makes any sense. Everything that up to that time was seen as pious appears suddenly as a betrayal of God; everything that was duty and commandment seems cynical and perverse. The seeds of a very different conviction begin to sprout: a certainty that the simple words of the man of Nazareth were immortal. But how can we get to that point?

What happens is that a youthful figure begins to speak from the tomb—on the right side, where consciousness dwells—and sends the women back whence they came: to Galilee. None of the words they had believed, none of the deeds they saw, has been revoked, lost, or contradicted, certainly not by Good Friday and absolutely not by the doings of the executioners. What Jesus was abides in God. That is the only thing that really enables us to live, and the only thing that outlasts death.

First Sunday after Easter

27. In White Garments

After the sabbath, as the first day of the week was dawning, Mary Magdalene and the other Mary came to see the tomb. And behold, there was a great earthquake; for an angel of the Lord descended from heaven, approached, rolled back the stone, and sat upon it. His appearance was like lightning and his clothing was white as snow (Mt 28:1-3).

Why should a scripture meditation only talk about things that by tradition and agreement can be considered universal knowledge? Why should we not once in a while dare to say what we ourselves think about a particular text, especially the narrative that is at the heart of the whole Gospel?

When we speak of faith in Christ, we usually have at least two things in mind. On the one hand there are the miracles and deeds that God did through Jesus Christ. They exist in and for themselves, and the implication for our life is that we must fulfill certain demands and adopt certain changes in our mental outlook. From that point of view, there is essentially a moral relationship of understanding and good will between our lives and the message about God and Jesus Christ. But the texts we read in the New Testament never say anything of the sort. In particular, this text about the resurrection of Jesus speaks of the mystery of faith in a very different way.

In all the reports of the resurrection, we are told that in the morning women went to the Lord's tomb and there saw one or several angels. Ever since I have been reading these texts, I have been asking myself, how can anyone see or hear an angel? No photographic plate, not even with the most sensitive chemical emulsion, would capture its image, and not even the finest recording device could receive its words. An angel can be seen only with the eyes of the heart, not with those of the body: It is not an optical effect, but a new beginning within. An angel's speech cannot be heard with the ears, but must be received in a very finely tuned rhythm of internal poetry, in a moment when our whole existence is stirred.

What does it mean to say that an angel has appeared? At least since the Middle Ages, it has been a beautiful and sensitive teaching of the Church that God gives each of us a special angel to protect us throughout life. To be aware of this angel is to know that we are so sheltered and safe under God's wings and God's mercy that even in the midst of anxiety and danger we feel a sense of peace and security. When do we feel our life protected and elevated, as if a bit of heaven came down to earth and surrounded us like a cloud of light? To feel, hear, and see the angel of God in our life means in particular that we are secure in our own existence. The existence of every human being is meant to be something special, personal, and utterly irreplaceable. This image of us that God made long before we were created is what we may call our angelic image. It accompanies us always. It warns us when we go astray, it leads us when we are about to get into trouble, it draws and directs us if we respond to it. Each of us bears in his or her heart such a secure knowledge of what God meant us to be. You may ask, what does the appearance of such an angel—the image of our being, the reflection of divine providence and protection—have to do with the experience of Easter morning? We would have to say that the people who believed in Jesus of Nazareth encountered their angels in the person of this man, so much so that under his gentle hands their own essential self was brought to awareness and made indestructible. When he touched the forehead of someone, that person's thoughts were brought into harmony and the self was formed anew. There must have been so much freedom, maturity, and enabling of life in the words of

Jesus that a powerful impression of the nearness of God, of God's support, and of the angel of God in our lives was audible and visible in them. If we think of it that way, it must have seemed to the handful of people, especially the women who followed Jesus to the hour of his death, that on Good Friday everything had been destroyed. It is so easy to crush the first beginnings of hope, which are so terribly sensitive, and probably there is no worse law on earth than this: That the most sensitive can be broken with the least expenditure of energy. It takes the blow of a hammer to crush a stone, but an accidental movement of the elbow is enough to smash a precious vase, and an incautious word suffices to destroy the soul of a human being. The arrangements on Good Friday had the systematic support of the powerful at all levels, so those events must have appeared final and irrevocable.

Only those who have seen that Jesus is everything to them and that a life without him is unthinkable will be in a position to experience an Easter morning. None of the high priests and none of the Pharisees saw the figure of an angel, on Easter or at any time after. Only the woman from Magdala and her companion did, according to Matthew's Gospel, just those two who could not and would not leave Jesus' grave, because in it rested far more life than in everything outside it. The earth will go on turning, the universe will continue its dance, but it is a single dance of death and sorrow and does not deserve the name of life. Only people who regard the tomb with complete conviction as the place of truth can find in the sunrise of Easter a new hope and a new faith. It is the miracle of this Easter day that what began in the souls of human beings through the message of Jesus of Nazareth can never be killed. On the contrary, it increases within us until it becomes our own conviction. That is what seeing and hearing an angel at the tomb means.

How does one see an angel descending from heaven, rolling away the stone from the tomb, and opening the chambers of death to life? It is a process that we ourselves can and must observe again and again, if we are believers. We have to see open graves in which our bodily eyes may well behold nothing but destruction and suffering. It must have been easy to see open graves in the desolate destruction of 1917 at Chemin-des-Dames before Verdun. It must have been easy when we looked at the television images of the Shatt-al'-Arab in 1988, a field of corpses slain by Iraqi poison gas. Where our senses see nothing but the violation of humanity, the faith of Easter must make it possible to behold the truth that over the life of every human being, invisible and yet shining like lightning, an angel of God is watching. When we see it, the earth quakes. It cries out against the crimes of humanity, it is restless like a sentient being under our feet, and it is not pleased that we soil it with bloody and wicked deeds.

The Gospel of Matthew says that angels have snow-white garments, and that may be the loveliest experience of the Easter morning: It is possible for the robe of innocence to be restored to every human being. In the Church, and in the language of the liturgy, we celebrate the white garments twice: at baptism and at first communion. Then often only the little girls wear them, but they are meant for everyone. They are a bit of childlikeness and unsullied existence and irrefutable truth. In the Book of Revelation, wearing this white garment is the sign of the elect, and that means all of us without numerical limitations. Seeing an angel means being touched to the heart by the always true, eternally living figure and message of Jesus of Nazareth. Nothing will kill him, nothing can oppose him; he goes before us, for he is our future and Galilee is the home of all hope.

If this is so, we must think again, and deeply, about everything we call faith. If this is so, it is impossible to say anything to another that is independent of our self, of our experience, and of the movements of our own heart that Jesus called forth. Unless we encounter the angel of God, we will be unconscious of our sisters and brothers and even of the Risen One himself on the way to Galilee. To put it another way: Only to the extent that we ourselves begin to live and experience what Jesus gave us will we sense, know, and be able to say in faith that Jesus lives with God and never dies and that death has been overcome through the power of love and of life itself. We are all love's children, and to her we belong.

28. The Emmaus Road

Now that very day two of them were going to a village seven miles from Jerusalem called Emmaus, and they were conversing about all the things that had occurred. And it happened that while they were conversing and debating, Jesus himself drew near and walked with them, but their eyes were prevented from recognizing him. He asked them, "What are you discussing as you walk along?" They stopped, looking downcast. One of them, named Cleopas, said to him in reply, "Are you the only visitor to Jerusalem who does not know of the things that have taken place there in these days?" And he replied to them, "What sort of things?" They said to him, "The things that happened to Jesus the Nazarene, who was a prophet mighty in deed and word before God and all the people, how our chief priests and rulers both handed him over to a sentence of death and crucified him. But we were hoping that he would be the one to redeem Israel; and besides all this, it is now the third day since this took place. Some women from our group, however, have astounded us: they were at the tomb early in the morning and did not find his body; they came back and reported that they had indeed seen a vision of angels who announced that he was alive. Then some of those with us went to the tomb and found things just as the women had described, but him they did not see." And he said to them, "Oh, how foolish you are! How slow of heart to believe all that the prophets spoke! Was it not necessary that the Messiah should suffer these things and enter into his glory?" Then beginning with Moses and all the prophets, he interpreted to them what referred to him in all the scriptures. As they approached the village to which they were going, he gave the impression that he was going on farther. But they urged him, "Stay with us, for it is nearly evening and the day is almost over." So he went in to stay with them. And it happened that, while he was with them at table, he took bread, said the blessing, broke it, and gave it to them. With that their eyes were opened and they recognized him, but he vanished from their sight. Then they said to each other, "Were not our hearts burning [within us] while he spoke to us on the way and opened the scriptures to us?" So they set out at once and returned to Jerusalem where they found gathered together the eleven and those with them who were saying, "The Lord has truly been raised and has appeared to Simon!" Then the two recounted what had taken place on the way and how he was made known to them in the breaking of the bread (Lk 24:13-35).

What these two people left behind them when they turned their backs on Jerusalem and started for Emmaus was the funeral pyre of all their hopes. Within the walls of the holy city, everything in which they had invested their hope had been destroyed. To them, the person of Jesus meant not just something, but the salvation of Israel, the fulfillment of all the promises. In his presence they had held it in their hands. Then they saw it destroyed, and not just by anyone, not even by an unfortunate accident, but by law and judicial process. To understand such a thing is humanly impossible, and the farther they got from Jerusalem the more they departed from the world in which their lives were lived and in which they had seen their future. Emmaus, in this sense, is a nowhere land, not a place to go, but a nothingness. Everywhere they go, Jerusalem will be there, but no one can exist within it. *That* is what it means to go to this village only sixty stadia distant; in actuality, the abyss of a whole world lies between.

From that point of view, it is important that these two have not stopped trying to understand what they have experienced. There is a kind of pain that is dumb, that conveys the feeling that no words are adequate or capable of expressing. Just to remain in communication with another in the face of the incomprehensible is a great deal, and often it is the beginning of faith. Then we can talk with one another, as we see in the most intense scenes in the Old Testament. There sits Job in front of his house, and he cannot understand anything, because suffering has crushed him. He cannot believe in God anymore, and he does not understand the things that have been said to him about God. After days of sorrowful silence, his friends speak to him, but they talk about the God they know. They say the things a pious Jew has to say, and they don't reach Job, because his experience is quite different. We in the Church are also inclined to deny experiences of this kind. We think it is not right to be so inconsolable and so despairing, now that God has been revealed in Jesus Christ. We go on sitting there, sounding like Eliphas of Teman talking to Job, until Job gets angry and says: "No doubt you are the intelligent folk, and with you wisdom shall die!" (Job 12:2). What he means is, you have wisdom, you know everything, but you know nothing about life because you protect yourselves against it with your talk. It will be a long time before God acknowledges this honorable, God-seeking Job, in a response not unlike that given to these two honestly searching people on the road to Emmaus. It is an experience we can only have when we take to the road. The world may be crushed, but we have the promise and assurance that we will find God and that God will accompany us, no matter where our steps take us. That is the beginning of the Easter experience: The Jesus we have come to know does not leave us, but instead goes with us in spirit, if for no other reason than because anything else is unthinkable.

The unknown companion on the road to Emmaus asks a question. "What are you talking about?" We are always inclined to see the questions addressed to people in the Old or New Testaments, whether by God or by Jesus, as somehow hypothetical: not questions, but really declarations or advice we are supposed to accept. In reality we ought to spend sleepless nights thinking about God's way of asking questions. They keep coming, these divine questions, and they are far more than declarations; they are a calling into question of the things that seem so certain to us. Among the things that appear inevitable are sorrow and despair. They cannot be refuted by counterarguments; we can only work through them by opening our mouths and letting our sorrow pour out all the words it has to say, again and again. We *have* to know, and it can be a long time before it becomes clear, when our tears become fountains and flow in cleansing streams. So Jesus' question.

Then the disciples on the Emmaus road come to a halt, and the motion of their advancing flight is stilled. In this moment something swells inside them and bursts out, "About Jesus of Nazareth!" They cannot comprehend that there could be anyone in Jerusalem who did not know and had not seen what had happened there. They have to explain it as best they can. Worst of all is the apparent legality and righteousness of the judgment that had caused so much wrong. How was it possible that their own high priests could misuse the word of God to murder a man who obviously came from God? How could the leaders of the chosen people bring themselves to the point of handing him over to the Gentiles so that they, the instruments of death, could carry out the sentence they had long ago decided upon? Nothing seems to make any sense; it is all utterly contradictory. It is not changed by the fact that there are rumors of hope from afar, even reports of visions. With their eyes full of tears, people cannot believe in angels; they cannot even understand themselves.

Yet Jesus calls his own disciples foolish and slow of heart to believe what the prophets had said. When we read this sentence, we skip ahead quickly, because we take it as a kind of early witness to the practice of giving scriptural proofs and the way the early Church quoted the "Old

Testament," interpreting it as applying to Jesus. It used every appro-
priate text that way: the psalms of lament, the Suffering Servant songs,
whole passages from the prophet Zechariah—but that is not the issue
here. Was it not necessary for the Messiah to suffer all these things to
fulfill the ancient prophecies? The true turning point of this story comes
when suffering is pushed to the extreme, to the essential. True, it was
no accident. It was ordered and decreed by law and paragraph. God
was called upon to refute Jesus' message about God. All that is true,
but now it is necessary to read the Bible from the beginning with new
eyes. When was it ever any different? *That* is what they have to
understand. Precisely because it was not an unhappy accident, they
have to see that Jesus was not proved wrong by being killed; instead,
he expressed and brought to life the conflict that is so clearly articulated
in every passage of the Old Testament.

His contemporaries saw Jesus himself as Jeremiah returned to life.
What did people do to Jeremiah? They threw him into a pit because he
called for prayers that King Nebuchadnezzar might come and destroy
the holy city of Jerusalem and the Temple along with it. That is just the
kind of thing Jesus said: "I will destroy the Temple." He did not desire
external religion, assured ritual, guaranteed formulae; he wanted living
human beings receptive to the Spirit and ready for life to begin. It is
the eternal conflict between a religion of externals and a religion of
experience, between prophet and priest, between the habitual repetition
of the traditional information and the explosion of something really
new. It is a mortal combat. When was it ever any different?

Others saw in Jesus the return of Elijah, and he really was like the
image of that great man in flight or struggling on Carmel against the
demonizing and idolizing of God by the power of fear. He had collapsed in the desert under the broom tree when the angel came to
strengthen him. Elijah walked to the mountain of God, Horeb, where
God appeared to him, as mighty as the wind and as soft as the words
of tender love, a sound of sheer silence. That is how God spoke to
Elijah.

How right Jesus was when he said to his opponents, in the words of
Luke's Gospel: "Woe to you! You build the memorials of the prophets
whom your ancestors killed" (Lk 11: 47). When they are safely dead,
you take their words and use them for your own purposes. Then you
know everything, you write it all down and teach it to the children. You
build temples and holy places as memorials to the murdered prophets,

but because you do not live in the present and lack the courage to do, here and now, what your learning could teach you, you are nothing but the children of the prophets' murderers. The struggle does not cease. Nothing in this story is an accident. Jesus was not proved wrong; he was affirmed in the witness of all the great figures of the Old Testament. What is Old Testament, and what is New? It is all the word of God, and it is always new. So Jesus lives through all time, and so we must begin to read the Scriptures not as the words of a God of the dead, but as words that are always renewing themselves for life. Nothing in them is fixed, for they are eternally in motion. Then we have an image that will never pass away: God is with us and calls to us, and not only us, but everyone.

This may be the oldest symbol available to human beings: sitting together and sharing a meal. It may be that this is the way we first became human, by sharing what we had gathered or captured with one another in order to be together—ancient experiences of solidarity and even of justice. One of the images Jesus used in his own day was that of a meal from which no one is excluded. He wanted to invite the outcasts, the people with whom others did not break bread. They broke rods over their backs instead, and lashed out at them to keep them away. Jesus wanted to invite them to the table of community under the heaven that belongs to all; and that, he said, is what God is like. This symbol will live, administered by priests but open to prophecy, to the life that is forever: a bread in which Jesus shows himself as never dead. That little bit of kindness will bring us close, that experience of our hearts on fire will set him before our eyes, and all the ways will turn back again, back from Emmaus to the place where our hopes had been destroyed.

Second Sunday after Easter

29. Forgive One Another

On the evening of that first day of the week, when the doors were locked, where the disciples were, for fear of the Jews, Jesus came and stood in their midst and said to them, "Peace be with you." When he had said this, he showed them his hands and his side. The disciples rejoiced when they saw the Lord. [Jesus] said to them again, "Peace be with you. As the Father has sent me, so I send you." And when he had said this, he breathed on them and said to them, "Receive the holy Spirit. Whose sins you forgive are forgiven them, and whose sins you retain are retained" (Jn 20:19-23).

Whenever people are able to forgive one another, there is a kind of miracle in our lives, because we are incapable of forgiving real guilt unless we see a vision, a dreamlike image like that given to the disciples in the upper room. It is a vision of wounds that are transfigured, of a life that cannot be destroyed, of a goodness that is not done away by death, and of a peace that cannot be torn from our hearts by any kind of violence. Without this image, every "I forgive you" is only an attempt and, even when it is well meant, it is often a powerless betrayal of oneself and of the other as well. We often try much too soon to say "It's all right," and "Forget it," and "Let's just drop it," and "Don't say any more about it. I forgive you. It's okay." What we really mean is, don't rub the old wounds any more; let's just let it be. But as long as there are real wounds that smart and sting, we should not be so quick to say, "I forgive you," because we do not have the strength to maintain it. Instead, if we really trust the other person to have enough insight and good will, we should try to discuss the matter together, to explain how much we have been hurt and why a thoughtless word or a careless action, perhaps even a deliberate injury, has caused so much pain. As long as the wounds have not healed, we do not have the generosity needed for forgiveness. We are asking too much of ourselves and, ultimately, of the other as well. It is possible that we may say, "I forgive you," and it is easy because the pain is not too great. Then saying "I forgive you" really means, "it was not so bad." But when something truly sticks in our craw and causes us pain, I could almost say that honesty is more important than love of neighbor. We cannot really say that, because truth and love cannot contradict each other, nor should they, but without truthfulness in all the things of the heart, people will not come together, not even under the pretense of forgiveness.

The vision from the upper room gives us a more profound insight into the origin and source of the energy that enables us to be kind to one another. This vision of the transfigured body of the Lord tells us that when forgiveness enters our lives, it is as if wounds could begin to be an aspect of human beauty and hurtful things done could start to make the other person lovable and precious, until the suffering that has been inflicted on the other ultimately becomes an unbreakable bond of fidelity, community, and deeper union. Only those who have experienced in their own bodies the miracle that we can live beyond pain and grow beyond our wounds can learn to forgive others in a greater joy of generosity. Perhaps one might say, Well, it was easier for Christ than for us. Perhaps. When another wounds us deeply and our feelings are badly hurt, what usually happens is that the injuries we have received are turned into a kind of chronic hurt, a sort of subliminal hatred, a suppressed or partly acknowledged desire for revenge.

The wounds we receive do not stick in our clothes, nor do they remain on the surface of our lives or bodies. Instead, they eat into our souls, and that is usually our worst problem: The foreign evil almost always becomes our own. Only people who are very good, as Christ was, can avoid letting pain pass from the body into the soul. Almost all of us will have to learn to grow beyond the evil in our own hearts, not only beyond suffering from without, but even beyond the need to cause pain to others. Only a deeper knowledge of what causes us to suffer will give us the strength to understand and soothe the disquiet in the heart of another. Ultimately, what we tell the other is then not merely, "I forgive you," but more deeply, "I understand in my own heart how you could do that. I would be ignorant of myself if I did not recognize what is going on inside you." It is only in a community of understanding that the barriers between those who give pain and those who are wounded can be eliminated and hands can reach across the abyss, ready to clasp and not let go.

We cannot forgive others for what comes to us like a foreign demand, an incomprehensible evil, something that has nothing to do with our own soul, so to speak. The most important precondition of forgiveness is that we see and know that in the other person's place we would not be an iota better or different; what is going on inside him or her is just like what is inside us. Only when we genuinely feel and know this can we put a stop to the cycle of revenge.

Therefore I believe that the concepts we in the Church ordinarily use to describe the mystery of forgiveness are inadequate. From time to time the Church's magisterium expresses its concern that Catholics no longer have proper respect for the sacrament of Reconciliation, meaning that there are not as many people going to confession as there ought to be. We are told that they prefer to go to psychologists or astrologers. When I hear that kind of talk about penance, I am inclined to think that the Church ought to begin by doing penance itself, institutionally and publicly. The language of forgiveness has been reduced to a juristic action that has nothing to do with motives or feelings or inner understanding and does not go after the roots of evil. It only asks about the facts that can be brought to light and then says the wrong is forgiven. This has for centuries made the sacrament of Reconciliation a powerless administrative process that has nothing to do with the soul. At this point something has to change if we want to restore seriousness and depth to the most dignified images of healing we have received from Christ. It is unworthy of our dignity to reduce our lives to simple bookkeeping, balancing the commandments in one column against our shameful deeds in the other. Nothing will change, and nothing about us will improve, until we begin to understand ourselves. Then we will have to understand that there is no evil we do to another that we have not already done to ourselves. We have to understand that we cannot utter a lie without betraying ourselves, and we have to feel the effect of lying in our own bodies before we can stop it. We have to feel in ourselves that with every immoral act we surrender a piece of our own dignity; otherwise we will never get away from it. We have to see that when we hate another we abandon some of our own lovableness and tread on our own self-esteem; otherwise we will never stop. Therefore the words of forgiveness, even if they are spoken by a priest to a so-called penitent, are never real and never truly effective unless there is, in the background, the sense of a relationship that allows the other to live and changes his or her motives through a more powerful experience of love and happiness.

For in fact it is only the happiness that grows out of love that teaches us forgiveness, and I think that it is only possible to experience even the sacraments out of the fullness of life itself. What the Mass or the celebration of the Eucharist is worth are things we learn in our human relationships with one another, and what forgiveness is worth is something we do not learn in some corner, not even if it is in the Franciscan church or the Church of St. George. But we can practice. We need, and can find in the heart of everyone, a great longing for a dialogue with one another that makes it possible to talk about the painful, hurtful, often forgotten dark corners of our own hearts and our own past—stuttering, hesitating, choking, crying, screaming, cursing, whatever—ultimately perhaps grateful, gentle, calm and, I hope, someday even laughing. Perhaps the Church made a mistake in thinking that this magnificent opportunity offered by Easter to forgive the things that human beings can do to one another should be delegated to one particular group, the priestly caste, and that they in turn should be restricted to the male sex. I think that the passages in the New Testament that speak of a universal priesthood are right. So we read also in Matthew 18 that the work of forgiveness does not belong to one official group, but every believer is capable of and called to forgiveness. Where any human beings truly talk with one another so that their very being is changed by the kindness and understanding of the other, the motives for evil collapse of their own weight. It is not with violence, good resolutions, or clenched fists that a life can be changed, and it is not with gritted teeth and an oath that this or that will never happen again that a human heart is changed, but in the happiness of being loved by another, it is not hard to be good.

Then, suddenly, we arrive at the things to be discovered in this dream-vision of the Easter day. Suddenly we find that it is the very wounds, both those given and those received, that make even the suffering caused by our own guilt lovable and precious to ourselves

and others, that wounds can be transfigured, and that finally we find nothing objectionable in the other person because of the traces of suffering caused by guilt, whether that of others or our own. On the contrary, it is there that we find the traces of the grace of God and discover many reasons to be thankful to the other for understanding and kindness and to God, who writes so straight with such crooked lines. Finally, everything that was is only the long way by which we become the persons we are: marvelous human beings as God sees us and desires us to be, and as we learn to see ourselves.

30. One Heart, One Mind

The community of believers was of one heart and mind, and no one claimed that any of his possessions was his own, but they had everything in common. With great power the apostles bore witness to the resurrection of the Lord Jesus, and great favor was accorded them all. There was no needy person among them, for those who owned property or houses would sell them, bring the proceeds of the sale, and put them at the feet of the apostles, and they were distributed to each according to need (Acts 4:32-35).

When we ask ourselves, in practical terms, what difference it makes whether we believe in eternal life and the resurrection of the dead, the answer can be found in the wonderful message conveyed by the risen Lord when he breathed on the disciples that Easter evening. He gave them the power to forgive one another and to forgive everything. We have to recall the things Jesus said in the villages and towns of Galilee. Scarcely anything was as important to him as that we should not insist on our own supposed or imagined rights, but should see that we are all

guilty before God and capable of the communion of boundless understanding. This attitude was so clear to Jesus himself, and he lived it in
his own life so much as a matter of course, that he did not want to hear
anything about the way we ordinarily rely on laws and our own legal
titles and calculate and assign and deal with one another about what
we have done wrong. That won't get us anywhere. We have to understand that all these rights and all this insistence on legality are only
effective when there is no community of love. Relying on one's rights,
anyone can be a good citizen, literally a righteous and upright person,
irreproachable and respected, but never a genuine human being capable
of goodness.

For that reason, everything Jesus said and thought was like revolution and anarchy, dynamite for all forms of institutional security. Jesus
thought that what mattered was to see what another person requires
when he or she stumbles, what that person's primary need is and how
we can accompany that person and help him or her to see it. That was
Jesus' concern. Oh yes, we all know the petty hypocrisy with which,
finally, one after another stands up and celebrates his or her own
generosity by saying, "I forgive you"—and all this is just a more refined
way of wielding the scourge of humiliation, disparagement, and sa-
dism. But that is not what Jesus meant. He wanted us to abandon every
form of claim on one another, in order that we could enter all the more
into dialogue. If we could only see what is happening in the other
person's heart, we would be that person's companion on the way. We
would no longer need to protect ourselves against each other. We would
give another our shirt, if necessary, and if he or she asked us to go a
mile, we would go two or three miles, or as many as necessary, at that
person's side. That was what people found so hateful about Jesus. That
was what they pilloried him for. It destroys everything that is otherwise
so secure in normal, public, middle-class life.

But just imagine that goodness is proved right because it supports
life, that life is validated because it cannot be throttled by death! That
means that, face-to-face with the Risen One, we can literally put away
all fear from us, that there are no more limits to our readiness to forgive.
As long as we are afraid, no matter how much good will we have, we
will not be able to forgive except in trivial matters. We will be anxious
to protect ourselves, to ensure our security, and we will bar our doors
and set up barriers against contact with others—limits well-formulated
in our civil laws, in the rules of decency and public morals—all the

things that give apparent comfort to human existence. But in this new situation we can be defenseless before one another and we can see that even the wounds that life gives us can be transformed, for God is stronger than fear, and God's truth is greater than law, while the power of love is limitless.

Luke writes a wonderful commentary on this in the Acts of the Apostles. Paralleling the universality of forgiveness, he speaks of limitless giving. One might say he is sketching an ideal legend here. Was early Christianity really like that? It doesn't matter. Luke is right in saying that true Christians should be like those he describes in Acts 4. You heard rightly: In the community of believers, there was no one in need, because all those who had lands and houses sold their property. That is the spirit of Jesus. To repeat, as long as we are afraid, we will cling to our property and be careful to secure legal title to it as protection against the unsuccessful, those who have nothing and can do nothing, those we think are unworthy to hold property. We will intensify our mad notion that, although two-thirds of humanity is starving, it is probably because they are worthless people, but we upright folks are working for our property and deserve to own it. The whole system works marvelously. That is the basis of our so-called civic life: We organize death, accumulate wealth, and wear out and restructure material things until we ourselves are turned into dust, cheap as dirt in the end.

The truth is that for a moment we have the offer of an inner freedom that will enable us to feel and suffer with one another and to share with one another. There would be no hunger or misery if we were not continually clinging to our good, bourgeois laws out of sheer terror. Until we accept the offer, we are in such a state that even the Church is called upon to justify these very titles, to acclaim and support the whole world order of bourgeois society in which God is the highest lawgiver and the instance that secures our claims to property and the "good life." Shouldn't we trust human beings to be more deeply and thoroughly endowed with fantasy, humanity, idealism, and generosity than with profiteering, greed, and organized egoism? What do we have to lose when we have been given a whole life again, a genuine and true life? There is only one precondition for living together in openness and without limitations: that we trust in the immortality and omnipotence of love. For love Christ died, and in love he is risen, so that we might live.

31. How Can We Believe?

Thomas, called Didymus, one of the Twelve, was not with them when Jesus came. So the other disciples said to him, "We have seen the Lord." But he said to them, "Unless I see the mark of the nails in his hands and put my finger into the nail marks and put my hand into his side, I will not believe." Now a week later his disciples were again inside and Thomas was with them. Jesus came, although the doors were locked, and stood in their midst and said, "Peace be with you." Then he said to Thomas, "Put your finger here and see my hands, and bring your hand and put it into my side, and do not be unbelieving, but believe." Thomas answered and said to him, "My Lord and my God!" Jesus said to him, "Have you come to believe because you have seen me? Blessed are those who have not seen and have believed."

Now Jesus did many other signs in the presence of [his] disciples that are not written in this book. But these are written that you may [come to] believe that Jesus is the Messiah, the Son of God, and that through this belief you may have life in his name (Jn 20:24-31).

How can we come to believe today, two thousand years after the disciples' message?

This question was already posed by the author of the fourth Gospel, well aware of leaving for the coming generations nothing but a little book about fifty pages long. How can something that is only writing, just human words, give other people hope and confidence that the message of the resurrection can lead them from death to life? This is not a historical question; it arises repeatedly in our lives.

We are told that we can believe in God when we meet people who love us so much that they bring a bit of heaven down to earth. But what about the great mass of people who have never had such an experience? The question recurs again and again.

We are taught that we can believe in God when we see how the wounds life brings can be transformed and when severe suffering becomes open to life. But what of those who have never had such an experience in their own lives? Are there not people who have never encountered anything like salvation or a healed life, whose lives apparently consist only of misfortune, and who seem to be called to experience a living death in the darker reaches of existence?

The fourth Gospel closes with a deeply disturbing saying placed on the lips of the Risen One: "Blessed are those who have not seen and have believed." It is possible never to have had such an inner vision of the overcoming of death, the transformation of pain, or the victory of love on earth with one's own eyes, and still there is in our hearts the longing and desire for this message to be true; otherwise we could not live, and otherwise life would not be life for us.

It is possible to believe others when they say they have had an experience like that the disciples told of having on that first night in the upper room. Another who was not present may be inclined to think it is only pious talk or mere wishful thinking, perhaps even a kind of callous blather that ignores the reality of suffering and death. We have a right to be mistrustful of the pomp of smooth words. So much nonsense has been spoken in the name of God, and God knows there has been too much glossing over of things here on earth. It is a good thing there are people like Thomas who can say, "Show us; until we see it, *we* are not going to believe," and who don't allow any faith to be imposed on them if it does not show how life can be restored in its core values, beyond all the damage and deadly wounds that have been done to it. Thomas saw and felt, but after him came a whole world that asked the same question, and it did not receive a new vision of its own.

What should we do when we have to acknowledge the differences between the visionaries, who entered into the light at least for an instant, and the people who never emerge from the shadows?

Someone once told me how he himself understood faith. He knew that he was severely ill, and the doctors could not give him a definite prognosis of the results of an operation he was about to have. But he tried to gather up the fragments of his life into a picture that he had more sensed than seen up to this point. He said, "If I am honest, all my life it was not so much that I believed as that I wanted to believe, and now, when I can see death more clearly than life, I really have no more strength to say that this or that is true. Talk about the meaning of life seems almost cynical to me, because I feel myself to be empty and meaningless, and I ask myself every day how long this can go on. But then I say to myself, my present condition of disease and weakness *can't* be a reflection of the real world. To say that what I see now is the genuine reality would be as absurd as if I were to expect a broken mirror to give a *true* reflection of some object or other. I can't expect that when I am full of fear and sorrow and weakness and powerlessness my reason or my feelings see the world the way it really is. So I tell myself there were at least a few moments when I was closer to faith. I can't say that I ever really believed, but those moments in my life were powerful enough—at least I think they were—that in them the mirror might have been put back together, and there might have been a chance to see things the way they are."

I think that is something like what the fourth Gospel means here. It is possible to trust those few people on earth who can see rightly. Even if things have never seemed clear and simple in our eyes, still we have the witness of these few, and the question now is what we will make of it, whether we will envy them and complain to God that we did not have the grace given to Thomas to see and to touch, or whether we say to ourselves, *one* person like Thomas is enough for centuries. Someone like that at least points out the direction life should take, which is right for us, too. That person at least saw the dark wall of earthly existence open for a moment, and a single instant in the light is enough to know.

Then there remains an experience that we can give to one another, beyond all differences and beyond the dividing power of suffering. That is what the fourth Gospel means in its conclusion. How truly we can believe in the resurrection of Jesus, and how close we are to a life beyond the grave, is shown to us in the power of forgiveness. As long as a pain really tortures us, we can try as hard as we want, but we will still carry a little of the need for revenge within us. No matter how much good will we exercise in biting it back, it will still gnaw at us, and we will only be able to forgive in a very weak way. Our heart is only truly free when we understand that we can grow beyond wounds and injuries. Some time or other, we will even see that the most valuable aspect of a human being, what is most beautiful in us as persons, is ultimately all those times in our lives that originally gave us a great deal of pain, but in which we have learned to go on living. Those things have been transformed into sources of understanding and even, finally, of goodness. That is what Christ shows us on the evening of the Easter day. Beyond suffering and pain, and beyond the desire for revenge, there is a power of life that brings us close to God and lets us speak words of forgiveness that are valid in heaven and on earth.

32. Healing Our Ills

Many signs and wonders were done among the people at the hands of the apostles. They were all together in Solomon's portico. None of the others dared to join them, but the people esteemed them. Yet more than ever, believers in the Lord, great numbers of men and women, were added to them. Thus they even carried the sick out into the streets and laid them on cots and mats so that when Peter came by, at least his shadow might fall on one or another of them. A large number of people from the towns in the vicinity of Jerusalem also gathered, bringing the sick and those disturbed by unclean spirits, and they were all cured (Acts 5:12-16).

It is a truth known from the earliest ages of humanity that no one can speak plausibly of faith in God unless that faith includes the soothing and healing of human suffering and need. In this story from Acts 5, we sense Luke's great hope and trust that in Christ's Church this knowledge would become reality. There is, for example, a characteristic difference between the ways in which John the Baptist and Jesus spoke about God. If we follow the Baptist's preaching, we find that the first requirement is to make a decisive change in one's own life and to apply one's will to carrying out works of repentance and moral renewal. We human beings can be good, if we only will. The man at the Jordan felt confident in this.

Jesus must have found it very hard to turn his back on this simple and genuine call to repentance. We do not know in detail what caused him to do so, but the whole picture is unmistakable. He must have seen us human beings as much more helpless, unfree, and miserable than John the Baptist thought possible. Instead of pushing people in the right direction with stringent and severe demands, Jesus thought it better to speak a very quiet and kind language directed to human hearts, until the shuddering terror in them could be quieted and people could find the way back to themselves and to the sanctuary in their own hearts that is the temple of God. There should be no more lost, no more outcasts, no desperate people, and only the power of trust should bear us up, as if we were walking on the open sea, back to the strand on the other shore. The human heart must not be further distressed and made uneasy by threats, demands, commandments, and laws. Instead, it should put itself in order and dare to live of itself.

It is no accident that we hear it credibly told of Jesus that in his presence people were healed, if not of all their diseases, at least of all kinds of afflictions and sufferings. It happened that people who had formerly been bent down stood up straight, that people who had never dared to use their own eyes and went through life like blind people felt themselves drawn into the sunlight and could begin to see the path before their own feet. Others, who until then had felt like lepers, disgusting in others' sight, dared again to seek the company of other people and believed in their own original beauty and dignity. Such were the works and the words of Jesus of Nazareth. Luke tells us here in the fifth chapter of his church history, the Acts of the Apostles, that he could never see and believe in the group that calls on the name of Jesus, the Church of Christ, except as one that proclaims this generous, healing message, a message so living and so strong that it is continued and confirmed in lived experience and realized salvation.

In the company of the apostles, people pursued by unclean spirits recovered their own identity. How much in our soul has been considered unclean when it is only part of ourselves! Before it could show itself, it was already censured and put under control, because it was said to be sinful, common, hideous, dangerous, indecent, rebellious, egoistic. But what if the unclean in us is only what is unfinished and waiting to mature? It could grow into its bloom and greatness, if only we could quiet the fear that continually stamps it down with the terror produced by a violent morality.

In our teaching, we still talk about an original connection between faith and health, sin and sickness; we even learn and teach that because of original sin at the beginning of human history, our ancestors were driven from paradise and sickness became the lot of our earthly existence. But we externalize this teaching, which could be so significant and wise, by giving a purely external sense to the idea of sin. Sinning means violating certain commandments, and thereby the mysteries of human existence become an easily enumerated catalog of eternally valid precepts. It is paradoxical that the morality of compulsion according to fixed models is itself the cause of a variety of illnesses, and that what is true in the depths of our being is ultimately twisted into neurosis. In essence it is not a matter of morality and trespassing on commandments when we speak of sin (in the singular); it is a question of how distorted and torn our hearts can be when we are afraid, when we are under the influence of fundamental mistrust of ourselves and the whole world, and ultimately of the basis of our whole existence. The opposite of faith is not vice or immorality or a morally weak will. The opposite of faith is the inability to trust because we are burdened with endless anxiety. It is from *this,* literally, that sickness comes. As long as we feel ourselves to be driven, outcast, gone astray in a strange and accursed world, we can scarcely expect anything but that we should feel ourselves in our very bodies as strangers, wanderers, people beset. Ordinarily we feel ourselves so constrained and divided that we try to accomplish everything without any regard for our own selves, until at the end our soul only makes itself heard in the symbolic language of dreams and the symptomatic language of bodily illness.

Ultimately, sickness is the final appeal to what is left of our reason that it pay attention to truths that we repeatedly deny, often with the best of intentions. The present image of the world is no help to us in this. Since the beginning of the modern era, we have learned a good deal about our bodies, but according to a model that is only partly correct. The physical world, including our bodies, is represented to us as a construction in space and time organized by natural laws: physical, chemical, and ultimately mechanical. We have supposed that disturbances within this system can best be repaired and corrected by the use of chemical, physical, or mechanical means. Whatever happens within this model is manipulable, but at the end of the twentieth century we can scarcely ignore the fact that the one-sidedness of this world picture has created countless new illnesses that we cannot manage as long as we remain enslaved to this perspective. First and foremost, religion should contribute to the achievement of critical alterations in this image of the world and of the human being, an image that is practically ignorant of the soul, scarcely takes any account of human feelings, and continues to explain us as machines, making our life itself a mechanism that can be planned, governed, and shaped. We give the least attention to what is most complex: what human beings are in themselves, as feeling, thinking, irreplaceable beings. We must admit that Christianity itself bears a fair amount of guilt for this externalization, and it is even, in a certain sense, this very scriptural passage in which we can see the origins of this situation.

In a metaphorical sense, it was wonderful. A man like Peter can heal people plagued by unclean spirits simply by being there. His mere presence heals, and it is his shadow, which so softly glides over those exposed to the sun's heat, that effects the healing by its cooling and soothing touch. These are marvelous metaphors, if they were understood that way. But the history of their effects looks quite different. It is not the *person* of Peter that heals, but Peter, the rock, as *official!* He does nothing more than stand there or pass by, and the healing takes place. That is how it happens that we in the Church no longer believe there can be any such thing as healing through faith. We even teach today in our religious instruction (and require that it be accepted as true) that Jesus' miracles are really continued in the Church's sacraments. No one is healed by them anymore, and they are administered in such a way that they induce practically nothing in the way of experience. They are routine and almost mechanical. We miss the most important thing, and we in the Church need to learn it again today from the alienated brothers and sisters of Christ who have nearly been driven to enmity. These are the psychologists, psychotherapists, psychoanalysts—people who attempt, patiently and slowly, to seek the displaced, the disturbed, the people who have been declared unclean, and to do this as Jesus himself did. It costs so much to bring human beings back to themselves. Ordinarily it does not happen by a miracle in the sense of a sudden explosion or something incomprehensible that falls from heaven; for us, miracles take much longer. They bear a higher human cost. But who taught us that the nonsense we regard as normal has to be that way, that we should pay fifty dollars or more for three-quarters of an hour of healing conversation with a psychotherapist and that outside that, we are permitted to go on living as before—mechanically, cleverly, diligently—until we are finished and have finished off other people as well, and we really cannot expect any more than that "healing" means going to some repair shop in which we are made fit again so we can carry on the remaining struggle of life? What we thus pronounce "normal" is certainly not humanity, and it has scarcely anything to do with the visions of Jesus of Nazareth!

The fourth Gospel managed to say that Jesus was the Word of God, and in him the Word of God is alive for us. Two thousand years after the man of Nazareth, should we not be able and willing to learn, in some form or other, that we ought to be saying words to another in which the wings of heaven touch the other person's soul and lift it up and carry it and cradle it until it attains a trust that is healing? Moreover, that human words are able to express images and dreams and the suppressed poetry of the heart in such a way that the heart is reshaped once again under their influence and becomes whole, and that we human beings can approach one another with such sensitivity and care that to touch another person would mean to lift one another into the light and to make visible the purity and beauty of our being? Two thousand years after Christ, we must honestly admit, we have to begin again from the beginning and learn every step once more, because we have lost the idea of who Jesus Christ was. A religion that does not heal is a religion of idle talk with nothing to say, and it is certainly not the religion of Jesus of Nazareth. A doctrine that merely recites its findings without communicating anything to human beings is precisely what Jesus wanted to overcome. Two thousand years later, everything will begin again from the beginning, or else it is at an end. What, then, does Easter mean to us?

33. The Quest for Humanity

I, John, your brother, who share with you the distress, the kingdom, and the endurance we have in Jesus, found myself on the island called Patmos because I proclaimed God's word and gave testimony to Jesus. I was caught up in spirit on the Lord's day and heard behind me a voice as loud as a trumpet, which said, "Write on a scroll what you see and send it to the seven churches: to Ephesus, Smyrna, Pergamum, Thyatira, Sardis, Philadelphia, and Laodicea." Then I turned to see whose voice it was that spoke to me, and when I turned, I saw seven golden lampstands and in the midst of the lampstands one like a son of man, wearing an ankle-length robe, with a gold sash around his chest. . . .

When I caught sight of him, I fell down at his feet as though dead. He touched me with his right hand and said, "Do not be afraid. I am the first and the last, the one who lives. Once I was

*dead, but now I am alive forever and ever. I hold the keys to death
and the nether world. Write down, therefore, what you have seen,
and what is happening, and what will happen afterwards" (Rev
1:9-13, 17-19).*

How is it possible to hope in the face of death and to believe against
the whole world?

This is the question addressed by the last book of the New Testament, which we call the Book of Revelation or the Apocalypse. An
apocalyptist is usually a person who writes the dark prophecy of the
end of the world on the walls of a given time and place, evoking visions
of catastrophe and destruction before the eyes of our spirits. For the
early Church, which produced the Book of Revelation near the end of
the first century, there was no more need to wait for catastrophes to
happen. For them, the central drama of human history had already been
played out when Life was crucified on Golgotha. Everything the
prophets had associated, centuries earlier, with the Day of the Lord—
dark clouds, the sun obscured, earthquake, and the trumpets of unend-
ing war—began and was concentrated in the hour when Jesus, crying
aloud, surrendered his spirit into the hands of God. For every believer,
this was the decisive moment in all of world history. Either the accusers
and the executioners were right when they declared that the humanity
and goodness the man from Nazareth tried to bring into this world were
utopian, or else what we call reason and logic and even proclaim to be
the unwritten law of history is itself convicted of being lies and
inhumanity, once and for all. After Good Friday, all those who believe
in Jesus Christ will have to see the world as it was depicted by the
Flemish painter Hieronymus Bosch at the beginning of the sixteenth
century: a gigantic hay wagon escorted by spiritual and secular worth-
ies, an enormous train of folly, greed, and buffoonery. From every side
people are rushing to heap hay on the wagon and to pile up booty of
nothingness. They are killing themselves, literally falling under the
wheels of this gruesome wagon that rolls with gathering speed toward
its end, the inferno.

The images of the world in the Book of Revelation are dark, and yet
they bubble up within the man living in exile on the little island of
Patmos like an overwhelming flood, reaching the surface, where they
can awaken other impressions and ideas about human beings and their
possibilities. These are visions such as we ordinarily find in the minds

of people whom we lock up in our hospitals and psychiatric wards. In general, these mentally ill people are those who suffer most from a world that is as cold as if we were in an expanding Ice Age. In these zones of experience, the images from the deepest layers of the soul emerge, as God gave them to us before we were created, images of hope, visions of the form that was really meant to be ours.

John on Patmos hears something like a loud fanfare behind his back, with the result that his whole perspective is changed. He must turn from looking outward and go backward, into his interior self. There he sees the figure of a human being, one who was awaited and prophesied centuries earlier. At the throne of God there has always stood the figure of one like a human being whose destiny is to descend to earth at the end of the ages, in a quest as paradoxical and desperate as the one attributed to the Greek philosopher Diogenes when he went about the marketplace in Corinth in broad daylight carrying a lighted lantern and illuminating the faces of those he met there. What's this nonsense? they asked him. And he stammered in reply that he was looking for human beings.

That, after all, is the question: Where and how we can find human beings. The figure of the human one appears to John's eyes in the light of the seven lamps in the ancient Jewish sanctuary. It is the vision of everything that lived in Christ: forgiveness of guilt, so that all the lost and strayed may find their way home again; words of kindness that are powerful enough to soothe all fear; signs of mercy and forgiveness, able to touch even those regions of the heart where soul and body are joined and the healing of sickness and helplessness can be accomplished. None of this is dead; it cannot die. It is possible to want to kill the light because its shining is painful to eyes that are accustomed to the dark, and yet the sun's rising cannot be denied.

The Sunday we celebrate at the beginning of every week has been, since the days of the early Church, the day of the *eternal* Easter morning, of the triumph of life over death. So there stands before John the figure of a human being who had been killed as the most miserable of all. He is dressed like a king, because in his mildness he will be the true ruler over the hearts of all people. He is dressed like a priest, because it is the power of his faith that calls down all blessings on our heads. In his hand he holds the key of death and the abyss, and he is able to impart a secret knowledge that is the key to all the times in human life and history. It is paradox enough that we receive the words of life with such contrary spirits. But apparently it costs us more than anything to think a bit of goodness possible in the face of fear, or to take hold of a simple life of truth in the face of the gigantic expenditure of endless struggle and obligatory exertion. The Book of Revelation thinks so, and it appears to be justified in the belief. The message of the reign of God, of God's nearness to each of us, is like the beginning of a final uprising of all contradictions.

In 1942, when it seemed to every reasonable person that Nazi Germany must be on its last legs, the war erupted in its full dimensions and in unimaginable rage, and in the next three years it consumed far more victims than those it had previously devoured. In similar fashion, the truth, the real apprehension of our genuine nature, will be what ultimately calls forth all the contradictions and oppositions within us. We have to fight through it, and we can, with the image of the Risen One before our eyes.

God can be infinitely close to us today. The only thing that may always stand in the way of God is the melancholy and dullness of our hearts, our lack of faith in ourselves and in God who accompanies us in time and eternity. That figure already stands before us, with the power to open and close the gates of hell, to conquer the death of the soul through the power of trust and goodness.

The eastern Church paints a true picture of the Easter scene. It says that between Good Friday and Easter, Jesus descended into the lowest regions of hell to take all the dead by the hand, to open their graves, and to lead each of them into the light by the touch of his hand. That the whole remaining history of the world may make something of that is the hope of Christianity and its fixed assurance, though all opposition may stand against it. But in the meantime, between the hideousness of reality and our hope for the divine, our lives are in motion, repeatedly fearful and yet full of confidence, repeatedly called into question and yet confirmed and supported, close to death and yet deeply entwined with life. For in time and eternity, we belong to God. God is the beginning and the end, and protector and companion on the way between the shores.

Third Sunday after Easter

34. How Do We Recognize God?

After this, Jesus revealed himself again to his disciples at the Sea of Tiberias. He revealed himself in this way. Together were Simon Peter, Thomas called Didymus, Nathanael from Cana in Galilee, Zebedee's sons, and two others of his disciples. Simon Peter said to them, "I am going fishing." They said to him, "We also will come with you." So they went out and got into the boat, but that night they caught nothing. When it was already dawn, Jesus was standing on the shore; but the disciples did not realize that it was Jesus. Jesus said to them, "Children, have you caught anything to eat?" They answered him, "No." So he said to them, "Cast the net over the right side of the boat and you will find something." So they cast it, and were not able to pull it in because of the number of fish. So the disciple whom Jesus loved said to Peter, "It is the Lord." When Simon Peter heard that it was the Lord, he tucked in his garment, for he was lightly clad, and jumped into the sea. The other disciples came in the boat, for they were not far from shore, only about a hundred yards, dragging the net with the fish. When they climbed out on shore, they saw a charcoal fire with fish on it and bread. Jesus said to them, "Bring

*some of the fish you just caught." So Simon Peter went over and
dragged the net ashore full of one hundred fifty-three large fish.
Even though there were so many, the net was not torn. Jesus said
to them, "Come, have breakfast." And none of the disciples
dared to ask him, "Who are you?" because they realized it was
the Lord. Jesus came over and took the bread and gave it to them,
and in like manner the fish. This was now the third time Jesus
was revealed to his disciples after being raised from the dead (Jn
21:1-14).*

Jesus' third appearance, at the lake, really takes place in our time,
not in that of the first disciples. When we hear their names, it is so that
we ourselves should add our names to the list and try to find and share
the same experiences in our own lives. For this is a story that intends
to say for all time how we can find Jesus as someone who overcomes
death and makes our lives rich.

We find the disciples at their daily work. It is unsuccessful, a long,
endless night of effort without result. How long such periods in our
own lives may last, we never know in advance, and often it takes a very
long time before we even notice how empty our nets are. If someone
asked us why we do all that, we would have to say with the disciples,
"We are all in the same boat, and we are all working. Some Peter or
other said he was going to do it, and we went along. Don't ask us why."

But night and the sea are unmistakable in biblical symbolism. They
indicate that we have neither a future nor any expectations. They mean
that in this mood we find everything dark, and the earth beneath our
feet and all around us is like an abyss. Years can pass this way. We don't
lack diligence or skill, and seen from outside it may look like a good
and well-rounded life, but we ourselves know better. We know how
empty and insubstantial this way of life is. At the latest, when the light
begins to dawn like a new sunrise, we have to draw a balance. It is as
if someone called out to us from the farther bank of the river to ask
what we have brought with us. Whenever God questions people in the
New Testament, the issue is to find the truth at the crucial moment. The
questions are often penetrating, and we pass many sleepless nights
unable to escape them. Usually we would give anything if we could
continue our pretense a little while longer. To the question of how we
are and what we have brought with us to eat, we will try to peddle all
the old stories. That is why it is so important that Jesus, before he asks

this question, addresses the disciples with a word that seems inappropriate: "Children." But it is immensely important. It is an address that assures the disciples: You can stop trying to be so important and pretending to be big and impressive. You are permitted to be honest.

It is said of the discipline that is now called psychotherapy and that perhaps, hopefully, one day will be the ordinary way in which people can relate to one another, that it consists of allowing a person to be a child again and to work through all the experiences of childhood. It is certainly true that we are only able to face truth when we can say anything at all without fear of censure or blame. What else can the disciples do? They have nothing. Their self-revelation is not meant to humiliate them; it is the beginning of a new life, truly the dawning of a sunrise from the other shore.

The figure whom the disciples at first do not recognize tells them, "Cast the net over the right side of the boat." We must interpret that as saying, try to take hold of your life deliberately, so that it will mean something. The right side is the one connected by the nerve paths in our brain with reason, conscious experience, and language. To throw the net on the right side means to go back through all the things that have been, clarify them, and take one's life in hand, no longer because others may do or pretend to do this, but out of inner conviction, directed from the other shore. When we do this, our lives are filled with meaning. But we ourselves must know what we are doing and for what purpose, and it makes an enormous difference whether we live in stolid and slavish obedience to other people or whether we listen to the voice from the other shore.

What do we know of God, and how can we recognize God? There is a paradox in this story: The disciples do not recognize Jesus when they are close to him, but scarcely is the net full before the disciple who loves him, far out on the lake, knows with certainty that "it is the Lord." Should we conclude that when our lives begin to be rich and we start to feel happy we can better sense how close to us God is? There are many sayings that we have learned from Jesus, and we can fulfil all of them as things imposed from outside, but who he really is, and that he really lives, we will certainly experience only to the extent that we are truly happy. This marvelous text even tells us that we can count the happiness: 153 fish! It is not a question of the precise number, but it is as if each of us has a particular measure of happiness, so that more would tear us apart and less would leave us empty. To experience this measure of happiness as something that can be counted and thereby to find oneself whole, full to the brim, seems to be the condition of recognizing God and knowing who Jesus is.

Christianity—and indeed, every form of religion—has often been accused of representing a kind of flight from the world, a dream of the farther shore. This is not true. There are people like John (and some part of them lives, thank God, in each of us) who can see intuitively, with their eyes closed. There are also people like Peter (and, thank God, we are somewhat like him, too) who, as soon as they hear what there is to see and know, throw themselves head over heels into the lake, with their tunics tied around them.

It is true that we can and should surrender ourselves utterly to this world. But without the knowledge of the other shore, it is an abyss that sucks us down into the depths. Of course, if it is certain that the distance is only a hundred yards, the water will sustain us, and the world is trustworthy. It is faith that teaches us how to live, and we must know the distance between us and what we hope to attain if we are to dare everything and abandon all security.

Christianity, and every other form of religion, has also been accused of devaluing human beings. If there is a God who is absolutely perfect, utterly omnipotent, and completely happy, what need is there for human beings, weak and poor as they are, with all their chaos of night, despair, and emptiness?

The truth is, as this text shows, that happiness is meant to be shared. It is surely true that the disciples find everything ready for them on the shore, already prepared, and for a moment one could suppose that they would not have needed to bring all those fish with them, because the meal is ready. But isn't that the way it is when we are happy? The decisive moments of our lives, when we literally sense a bit of heaven on earth, are not at all those in which we ourselves could have contributed something. They are the moments in which we find or discover something like a grace, and it does not devalue us or rob us of our dignity—on the contrary. In the feeling of gratitude, all our own abilities and everything we bring with us enters much more richly into the whole.

What the disciples on the lake could not accomplish, or only with great effort—hauling in the net—can be done from the shore by a single person, by Peter alone. Nothing excessive needs to be said about this.

It is not at all different from our ordinary everyday life. It is no different from any Mass that we celebrate together. We bring with us all these experiences of suffering and emptiness, need and death, until we hear the call that is addressed to us and directs us to live rightly, and we return to where our life is, the place from which all the questions begin and where our wealth abides. But then it happens, as in this picture, that Jesus comes again, no matter how present he may be to us; he comes, breaks the bread, and remains with us. And none of us dares to ask, "Who are you?" because we know: It is the Lord.

There is a form of trust and love that is damaged by constant examination and demands for reassurance. There are points of contact that remain valid beyond all doubt. That is what the early Church prayed for when it repeatedly called on the Lord in his own words: "Maranatha: Our Lord, come!" We do this in the symbols of the Eucharist, and we bear it as hope in our hearts. There will be a dawn when the boat of the sun reaches the farther shore. The Lord will stand there waiting for us. He will fill our empty hands and teach us to see our life as a race that is coming to its end, with a rich prize awaiting us because we have made our contribution to the blessing of the world.

35. Do You Love Me?

When they had finished breakfast, Jesus said to Simon Peter, "Simon, son of John, do you love me more than these?" He said to him, "Yes, Lord, you know that I love you." He said to him, "Feed my lambs." He then said to him a second time, "Simon, son of John, do you love me?" He said to him, "Yes, Lord, you know that I love you." He said to him, "Tend my sheep." He said to him the third time, "Simon, son of John, do you love me?" Peter was distressed that he had said to him a third time, "Do you love me?" and he said to him, "Lord, you know everything; you know that I love you." [Jesus] said to him, "Feed my sheep. Amen, amen, I say to you, when you were younger, you used to dress yourself and go where you wanted; but when you grow old,

you will stretch out your hands, and someone else will dress you
and lead you where you do not want to go" (Jn 21:15-18).

When we look back on our lives to this point and ask who we are and what is the meaning of all we have done, we will probably discover that there have been particular turning points in our development in which the real meaning of life is concentrated. These junctures and turning points are almost always those moments in which we felt ourselves most challenged, and it seems that every step in our process of maturing is identical with secret questions addressed to our being, to us as persons. That is how we should understand this dialogue between Jesus and Peter. These are stations in a chain of questions that are not posed in a single moment, but through the stages of a whole life; Peter stands as a representative of that process. The content of all the questions points fundamentally to a single one: the question of the capacity and the nature of our love. Whenever God probes us, the questions are disturbing and incapable of final answers; they beset us day and night and can never be dismissed. In youth it may still seem as if we could give relatively clear and self-confident responses to such questioning. We think that we know ourselves, we are fairly confident in our abilities, and our own education and notion of the world teach us that it is the sign of a proper man or woman that they can give a concise and conclusive account of themselves. So Peter says here, "Lord, you know that I love you." And he believes it himself. Between the statement and the person there is no room for doubt, anxiety, or insecurity.

Of course we cannot ignore the fact that in this passage the questions God poses with regard to our life also have to do with the founding of the Church. The dialogue on the shores of Lake Gennesaret takes place after Jesus' death and resurrection, at the original scene of his work and his discourses. In a sense it is a late, mysterious, sweepingly visionary language on which the Church is founded. But then it is more than astonishing, it is a reversal of everything we know, when as the fundamental question, the legitimation of everything that is known to us as Church and as the Church's leadership, we hear: "Do you love me?" Every other human group is founded on the strength of its leaders. The leader is the one who, by the influence of sheer power, is most persuasive in uniting the largest possible groups of people under the leader's orders. Powerful, effective, clever, confident planners and goal-directed personalities are the shapers of world history. They are identified with skill and success. This is the case in every nation, in every interest group, in every youth gang on the streets. But Jesus is supposed to have shown himself to the spirits of his followers one early morning at sunrise on the shore of Lake Gennesaret, and he said that in his Church only those can be considered leaders who are outstanding in love; for love is the only thing that in the mind of Christ can legitimately have power over human beings. It is a language that reverses everything that these concepts otherwise mean.

"Do you love me more than these?"—That is a question stated in a context of competition and comparison. In other cases, we can establish by certain criteria who is better or who appears to be more powerful in the sense of external abilities, but when Jesus asks about love in a comparative sense, the question sounds absurd. Can anyone say "I love" and add "more than so-and-so"? Is it not a contradiction of the very essence of love to make it something that can be compared and measured, the object of competition? It seems that Jesus wanted—by the way he framed his question—to seize and overturn the whole system of thought and all the preconditions that we normally set for ourselves. In the end the issue is not whether Peter loves *more,* but whether he understands at all what love is.

Our modern languages are impoverished in their attempts to express the most important things in human life. For the whole spectrum of human affections, we only have one little word: *love.* We can differentiate a little, and within this scope of human encounters there is often a distance like that between heaven and hell. We say, "I love you," or "I like you," or "I am fond of you," and so on. In New Testament Greek, a distinction is made between *agape,* the love of Christians that governs their relationships with one another, and *philia,* the love of friendship between persons. Jesus asks first about the former, the love that determines our behavior toward one another, the Latin *caritas.* It would be something, even something great, if we could learn the kind of sensitivity that would prevent us from hurting one another and allow us to help one another to be and become what we are. Jesus asks his disciple twice about this, and is answered in terms of the love of friendship. He seems to want to say, "Lord, I have no guarantee that I am doing everything right, but I am aware of my feelings, and I want to say that you can look into my heart, and you know that I am most affectionately attached to you, that I am and want to be your friend."

For many of the decades of our lives, this answer will suffice. It is worth a great deal if we can believe in our own motives. Whatever mistakes we may then make, including even misdeeds and guilt that we may incur, there remains an indestructible center in which we can say, "All that was done for the sake of love; I meant well by it." We feel uneasy, however, when Jesus addresses the older, more mature Peter who has grown in self-knowledge with the question that tests even this conscious friendship. Now Jesus himself states the question as: "Are you my friend?" That is: Do you really love me in the sense of personal affection?

It looks at this point as if Peter is stripped of everything, and it seems to me that this questioning coming from the mouth of God, this growing insecurity in one's own unshakable confidence in the sense of this Gospel presupposes such a measure of prudence, goodness, wisdom, and understanding in relationships with other human beings that it is only on this basis that one might be able to say what, according to the mind of Jesus, a leader in the Church is and should be. While in the realm of politics the self-confident types may have the upper hand, in the Church of Christ it should be the prudent, the gentle, the patient. When we look at this Gospel, we ought to ask what we really want and what we have made of Jesus' message. With reference to Peter's role as vicar, as early as the eleventh century, under Pope Gregory VII, the papal role as vicar of Christ on earth was combined with an absolute claim to truth, and not long afterward Pope Innocent III felt himself able to state the power of Rome in words: Every cleric must obey the Pope, even if he commands something evil, because no one is lord over the Pope. At this point, there is no longer any distinction between power and truth. Naked power declares itself to be truth. Then the centrality of the powerful individual becomes the basis and source of every imaginable right and law. The leader is the supreme judge. That is how the Roman emperors thought, and the same idea penetrated the Church of Rome, but how far removed it is from the gentle direction of human beings by nothing except the magical power of love! Jesus tells us in the fourth Gospel how he saw it: "I know each person by name." In the power of love, one learns to recognize the essence of the human being so well and to value it so highly that no external guidance is needed and no pressure of command or compulsory obedience must be applied to people. Instead, the one who has listened long enough can utter what is in the human heart. Then they do not follow some stranger, but themselves, and that is what the Church should be.

As long as we are young, we are active, busy accomplishing things, having our way. The more we mature in the things of Christ, the fainter are his questions, to the point that we can scarcely hear them; but at the same time our life becomes more and more sensitive, and obedience begins to ripen from within. This balancing process is a type of guidance, just as the sun guides when it floods the flowers, leaves, trees, and the eyes of human beings. It is more powerful than any force on earth; it raises things up, lifts them to the light, opens them to its warmth, and the energy that encourages development is the only guidance there should be in the Church of Christ. Jesus' question, "Do you love me more than these?" is one that Peter cannot answer. He will always, and ultimately with his whole being, have to say: "Lord, you alone know what I am." It would be the greatest happiness on earth to be able to know ourselves as God knows us.

Fourth Sunday after Easter

36. Called by Name

"Amen, amen, I say to you, whoever does not enter a sheepfold through the gate but climbs over elsewhere is a thief and a robber. But whoever enters through the gate is the shepherd of the sheep. The gatekeeper opens it for him, and the sheep hear his voice, as he calls his own sheep by name and leads them out. When he has driven out all his own, he walks ahead of them, and the sheep follow him, because they recognize his voice. But they will not follow a stranger; they will run away from him, because they do not recognize the voice of strangers." Although Jesus used this figure of speech, they did not realize what he was trying to tell them.

So Jesus said again, "Amen, amen, I say to you, I am the gate for the sheep. All who came [before me] are thieves and robbers, but the sheep did not listen to them. I am the gate. Whoever enters through me will be saved, and will come in and go out and find pasture. A thief comes only to steal and slaughter and destroy; I came so that they might have life and have it more abundantly" (Jn 10:1-10).

When people in the ancient world heard someone talking about a good shepherd, they thought of the national leader, the king, and his power. It was he who held the staff in his hand, who led and guided the community of all those subject to him. Without him, they were nothing. He was their head, their center, and their heart, so that no command was valid unless it came from the king, and no word was holy unless it came from the one in power. For centuries and millennia people bowed in the shadow of the uplifted hands of the rulers and in obedience to them enjoyed peace, justice, and something like happiness that was simply taken for granted.

An incredible turning point was reached when a little group of former nomads who had been forced into the Nile delta after centuries of oppression recalled the heritage of their ancestors and escaped by night to seek freedom. With a clear no and a vigorous protest, Israel spoke in the prayers and songs of its psalms:

> The Lord is my shepherd; I shall not want.
>   In verdant pastures he gives me repose;
> Beside restful waters he leads me;
>   he refreshes my soul.
> He guides me in right paths
>   for his name's sake.
> Even though I walk in the dark valley
>   I fear no evil; for you are at my side
> With your rod and your staff
>   that give me courage.

It is only of God that people may say such things, and no human being should dare to grab the spotlight from God with presumptuous orders or the unwisdom of arrogance. What is said *about* God merges naturally into an address *to* God, because God is not some object about which we can speak. God is always a partner for Israel, the eternal, ever-present, accompanying Person. Under the shadow of that Person, everything comes to its true form, especially the breath of freedom and the greatness of the human calling.

In the text of the fourth Gospel, Christianity seeks to describe what people experienced in Jesus of Nazareth, and though these experiences are different, there is nothing in them that can detract from what had happened in Israel. On the contrary: Jesus' whole desire was that people should once again find immediate access to God as their Father, their protector, the focus of their trust, love, and confidence. Apparently we need people like this who can open the way for us against the gigantic burdens of inhumanity.

When we at the end of the twentieth century hear these texts about the one who watches or guards the gate, we cannot help thinking of one of the grimmest anti-fairytales of our time, Kafka's novel, *The Trial*, which contains the narrative called "Before the Law." Before the law stands a doorkeeper. This is a parable describing how people under the influence of fear are prevented from finding access to the justification of their own lives. They are continually being ordered because of this or that regulation to do things that they do not intend to do and that they scarcely understand. No matter what they do, they are always wrong, always outsiders, always unjustified, because their lives are always blocked by another who knows better, whose ideas are different, who is more correct, a scary monster. How old do we have to be before we can put an end to this phantom? Kafka tells us that we will die of it, as long as fear has power over the human being. In the end we will find that we have knocked at the right door, but how do we gain entry? It is a life-and-death question.

Jesus wanted us to have access to our life in the hands of God. When he speaks of a doorkeeper, he is not thinking of a toll booth that we have to pass under the eyes of some foreign official; rather, our own heart is an organ sensitive enough to know when we should throw open its door and when we should not, and this is the true criterion for our dealings with other people, especially when God is the subject. In this passage it is clear what really happens in that situation and what it all means. If the door of the heart opens freely and of itself, like the petals of a flower in the morning light, we can be sure that God is at work in us. But when hidden paths and detours are needed, when the door is broken down by brute force, we can be certain that no matter what fine words are used to describe the process, there is nothing of God in it.

The question is, what is the desired end? All the rulers of nations want to organize large groups of people, to rule and govern them. They are always responsible for everything, they have to do everything on behalf of *all*. That is just the opposite of what began in Israel's faith and was continued in the person of Jesus: the concern for each individual, for *his or her name,* because each of us exists only once in all the world, and God wants to call each of us by name.

The fourth Gospel summarizes here in a few concise words what is broadly described in the other Gospels, especially in their miracle stories. People are often in such a condition that they don't even know how to say their names or who they are. Their own consciousness, their feeling for themselves, their ability to determine the course of their own lives, has been thoroughly destroyed in them. How often did Jesus lay his hands on such people so that those impulses began to be felt again in their hearts and heads, as if a whole troop of evil spirits had been driven out and people were restored to themselves? How many roads must one walk with other people before they find themselves at home?

Jesus interpreted his work as a shepherd in just that way: to accompany every human being to the place where he or she is at home. This requires mutual trust. Each of us is fundamentally aware whether others are concerned for us or merely want to use us, whether there is interest in our lives or whether we are only to be made pawns in some game for the sake of something else: power, prestige, prominence. Leading people by the hand is really not the same as pushing, forcing, correcting, and ordering them. People can only be led by awakening their inmost selves and bringing to light something they have long known but deeply hidden, so that they can put it into words and recognize it again. Such a shepherd never comes from far away and is never a stranger to our natures, but speaks our very own language. That is what Israel desired when it chose as its core commandment: "You shall worship no strange god." Nothing that does not enter your heart as something long known and trusted comes to you from God. So it is with God, and so it is among human beings. Only in this way can our freedom be preserved. It is a dialogue of trust and love that the fourth Gospel describes, and Jesus' whole way of life is its epitome.

It is easy to see why the disciples did not understand all these metaphors. Even at the end of the first century of our era, at the time of the Johannine churches, there seems to have been a question about how to call on the example of Jesus in determining how people were to be led. In the future, Jesus would be the measure of what we do with one another, including what we do or allow to be done to us in the Church. A shepherd's staff can be used in different ways, either according to the model of the ancient Pharaohs and those who ruled by divine right, or according to that of Jesus' shepherding rod. The crucial alternative for Jesus' disciples is established in Jesus' words, even to the end: "The kings of the Gentiles lord it over them and those in authority over them are addressed as 'Benefactors'; but among you it shall not be so. Rather, let the greatest among you be as the youngest, and the leader as the servant" (Lk 22:25-26). That is why Jesus can say here in the fourth Gospel, "I am the door." There will be no way to approach other people other than his. It is possible to increase the size of human groups by force, to gather taxes, to augment the apparatus of administration, but we can only encounter people as Jesus did if we call them by name, saying who they are, what life is in them and, much more important, what that life can be.

37. God's Dwelling

"I am the good shepherd. A good shepherd lays down his life for the sheep. A hired man, who is not a shepherd and whose sheep are not his own, sees a wolf coming and leaves the sheep and runs away, and the wolf catches and scatters them. This is because he works for pay and has no concern for the sheep. I am the good shepherd, and I know mine and mine know me, just as the Father knows me and I know the Father; and I will lay down my life for the sheep. I have other sheep that do not belong to this fold. These also I must lead, and they will hear my voice, and there will be one flock, one shepherd. This is why the Father loves me, because I lay down my life in order to take it up again. No one takes it from me, but I lay it down on my own. I have power to lay it down, and power to take it up again. This command I have received from my Father" (Jn 10:11-18).

Where does God dwell? If we ask the various religions, they will give very different answers:

"God dwells in the beauty of all things and living creatures in nature," say the Hindu.

"God dwells in the depths of your being when you sink down there to the place where the flood of your heart is at rest and everything is wholly transparent, to the deepest depths," answer the Buddhists.

"God is beyond the heights of the firmament that encloses the whole earth, whose steel-blue dome is infinitely high above us," say the Muslims.

"God is our companion and our goal on the way to a common humanity, a world brotherhood and sisterhood of all nations as parts of one single people," answer the Jews.

We Christians could say all of this, and yet we add to it a remarkable and central experience of our own: Only when we encounter another human being in whose companionship we discover our own true nature do we find God. That is what we learned in the company of Jesus, with whom we could believe in God as his and our Father. Only in the company of a person in whom we can trust, unshaken by doubt and fear, are all the other answers of the religions valid for us. Without such an experience, the things of the world around us would remain empty and strange; they would absorb the alienated parts of our soul as separate and chaotic elements. Only in the company of love does the world acquire its unique poetry and allow itself to be penetrated by an endless song. Without such an experience our own hearts would be like restless, turbulent seas, constantly in motion above an impenetrable abyss. Only in love does our heart achieve rest and clarity, becoming a mirror for God's face. Without the experience of a human being at our side whom we can trust completely, God and heaven would be infinitely far from us, and heaven's silent spaces would offer more terror than consolation. But whenever a human being is close to us in love, heaven comes down to earth and is so close we can touch it. Only love teaches us to trust other people without limit and to take the road with them to our common goal, without separation or enmity.

Christ showed us this possibility in the image of the good shepherd: What he had begun in us could go forward, and we could be shepherds to one another, companions on the way. It involves the wonderful capacity that Christ described as his way of shepherding: the ability to call each member of the herd by name. For he knows each one, and so it hears his voice and knows him as the leader and companion of its life. We can say nothing more beautiful about the relationships of human beings with one another than that they succeed in calling each other by the word that is eternally alive within them. Not one of us would exist in this world if God had not first whispered something unutterable over the dust with the breath of eternity. By the power of love, our ears are able to hear this quiet word. Our eyes, opened by love, are able to behold the mysterious figure that the word called into existence, and our lips are able to utter it with the utmost tenderness. Whenever this happens, everything in our heart answers, and the whole world becomes one, and our whole being is open to God.

So it must have happened in the history of religion that the early Church did not invent the image of the good shepherd, but transferred it from the sun-worship of the Mithras cult, as if to say: That is just the way it is, that is what we have learned. When we accompany one another on the path of life and thus tread in the footsteps of Jesus, we can give one another all the warmth and light of the sun, because our hearts are filled with brightness. We can live what Christ entrusted to us in the Sermon on the Mount: When your sister or brother asks you to go a mile with her or him, go two instead. Christ certainly meant that our shyness and shame will not let us trust ourselves to say how much we need and what we lack, and yet we are in a position to understand more deeply and even to sense and to fulfil the unexpressed longings behind those we are capable of uttering. We can be companions for one another without limit. Our call is endless, and the breadth of the world is boundless. Its horizon is eternity.

Someone may say, what can we human beings really do? One little deadly puff and we no longer exist. Which of the essential dangers of life can we alter?

This is what we can do for one another here on earth: We are not the basis of confidence, it is true, but with the trust we give, with the love in us, we can awaken, call out, and cause to grow in the heart of another so much of the trust and love that God has put there that no power on earth can kill it again. For in us dwells an eternal life. And Christ is right: There will never again be a moment, not even in death, not even in the collapse of our earthly existence, when we must feel ourselves abandoned. God will always be with us, and wherever we accompany one another, we make tangible the certainty that we have in faith that points us to the ultimate basis of our whole existence.

The question remains how much the image of the good shepherd applies to our relationships with one another. The fourth Gospel presents us with two possibilities. There is the bitter word of the prophet Ezekiel on the shepherds of Israel, "The wind tends my flock," and the cynicism of the ancient rulers of Rome, who were also called good shepherds. The one group ruled with indifference and the other with violence. We are always in danger of letting our relationships get into that same swing of the pendulum, either making tyrannical demands on others or turning away and declaring them unworthy of further notice. But this art of finding our way to the center of another human being's heart—and so to the center of the world, the heart of God—that is the whole art of living.

If someone were to ask us what our existence was all about, what we have done and why we lived, we will certainly have to list all the ways we have failed out of weakness, cowardice, ignorance, laziness, and how we have fallen short in this and that. But let us hope that we can also answer that we have tried, at least tried, to live something like the image of the good shepherd for those around us. For we are all sisters and brothers in the hand of the eternal, divine shepherd who goes before us and whom we follow in every work of sisterly and brotherly love.

38. A Generation of Prophets

Then Peter stood up with the Eleven, raised his voice, and proclaimed to them, "You who are Jews, indeed all of you staying in Jerusalem. Let this be known to you, and listen to my words. These people are not drunk, as you suppose, for it is only nine o'clock in the morning. No, this is what was spoken through the prophet Joel:
'It will come to pass in the last days,' God says,
*   that I will pour out a portion of my spirit upon all flesh.*
Your sons and your daughters shall prophesy,
*   your young men shall see visions,*
*   your old men shall dream dreams.*
Indeed, upon my servants and my handmaids
*   I will pour out a portion of my spirit in those days,*
*   and they shall prophesy.*
And I will work wonders in the heavens above

> *and signs on the earth below:*
>   *blood, fire, and a cloud of smoke.*
> *The sun shall be turned to darkness,*
>   *and the moon to blood,*
>   *before the coming of the great and splendid day of*
>   *the Lord,*
>   *and it shall be that everyone shall be saved who calls*
>   *on the name of the Lord.'*
> *You who are Israelites, hear these words. Jesus the Nazorean*
> *was a man commended to you by God with mighty deeds,*
> *wonders, and signs, which God worked through him in your*
> *midst, as you yourselves know. This man, delivered up by the set*
> *plan and foreknowledge of God, you killed, using lawless men*
> *to crucify him. But God raised him up, releasing him from the*
> *throes of death, because it was impossible for him to be held by*
> *it. . . .*
>
> *All who believed were together and had all things in common;*
> *they would sell their property and possessions and divide them*
> *among all according to each one's need. Every day they devoted*
> *themselves to meeting together in the temple area and to break-*
> *ing bread in their homes. They ate their meals with exultation*
> *and sincerity of heart, praising God and enjoying favor with all*
> *the people. And every day the Lord added to their number those*
> *who were being saved (Acts 2:14-24, 44-47).*

The speeches that Luke places in the mouths of Peter or others of the Twelve in the Acts of the Apostles do not contain the words spoken at the time in any historical sense. Instead, they are ideal formulations of the things that *must* have been said then. These words contain the description of how faith in Christ was formed and articulated after his death. The speech is about us as Church, but the question is, who are we before we become believers? That very question displaces everything, so that to answer it, we have to talk about Christ. But to understand either one, we have to put aside all of our ordinary, familiar ways of thinking and hear as if for the first time how surprising the things spoken of here really are. Peter addresses us, and for the moment we think that we know what this is all about. This is the first man of the Church, the leader of the apostolic council, thus the kernel, at least, of what would become the Pope of Rome. When he speaks we are faced with issues of authority and obedience, teaching office and submission, hierarchy and laity; divine authority is connected with his title. So we believe. We have to be very surprised when we learn that he is speaking of exactly the opposite. This is about the Church, about *us,* but the real subject is God, and how God acts at the end of the ages. That is what we are really hearing. Here is the birth of a religion as religion was meant to be, a utopia built on truth, and it consists in God's bringing to pass what the prophet Joel had foretold: God will send forth the Spirit on *all* people. Hence even Peter's address in the Greek, "You men who are Jews," is no longer correct (and the English translators have reinterpreted it), because the Spirit of God rests equally on women and men, and the distinctions of the patriarchal social and religious order are invalidated. Now there will be an end to divisions not only between men and women, but also between owners and slaves. The foundations of the whole ancient structure are no longer solid. God is interested in all people, even and especially those whom others liked to keep in their places as servants. For that is the meaning of the divine Spirit, and the way to experience it is that people begin to understand that they are free, themselves born of the Spirit, and there must be an end to a situation in which one person stands before another and says, "I know who you are; in fact, I know what you ought to be; still better, I know what your whole life should look like, because I am the truth for you and you have to listen to me, since God is speaking through me." It is just the opposite. God has something to say in and for each individual, and God has need of every life in order to accomplish the divine self-communication to the whole world. Then there are no more authoritarian hierarchies, but only people from whom something new is breaking forth of itself, and each of them speaks with the power of prophecy fulfilled; each one's face is immediately present to God.

There had once been something like that in antiquity. People thought that a human being could be born of the divine spirit, and such a one was a king, a sovereign, totally autonomous, determining what he was and did. The foundations of this idea were laid in ancient Egypt, and it maintained itself for over four thousand years in the heart of the Western world. The king was an absolute ruler, a monarch; the world rested on him, and his whole kingdom was at his feet. It took us at least until the French Revolution, two hundred years ago, to shake off this idea, but we should have understood two thousand years earlier that it is not *Christian* to make human beings into obedient subjects. Each of us is something royal, each of us is born of the freedom of the wind, the beauty of the sun, the breadth of the heavens, the openness of the world, and each of us stands between time and eternity, finity and infinity, and is a unique and marvelous being. Each of us possesses our own worth and dignity, which no one can take from us. *Each* of us is the sovereign of our own life. Who else?

Joel himself had guessed that the birth of a new human type and a new fundamental attitude was only possible as a result of the collapse of all the systems of order. The sun will sway and the moon be darkened. Day and night, everything that formerly seemed to give security and support will collapse, but only from the destruction of everything that previously aided our orientation can there emerge what we can be. It is precisely this collapse of everything that happens to those who know that God is breathing in them and through their mouths. We can think of examples of what happens when people begin to think and feel for themselves and are not constantly thinking against their own feelings or experiencing their feelings as a betrayal of their thoughts; instead, thoughts and feelings begin to spark each other. It is a wonderful experience: "Your sons and your daughters will prophesy." Then a generation will grow up that does not stop believing in itself at the age of fifteen because they are taught, "All the things you have hoped for and desired and longed for are just the impulses of puberty; you have to forget all that and grow up. What we need are not visions, but fidelity, reliability, accuracy. That is the key to efficiency. You have to stand with both feet on the escalator to success and let yourself be carried slowly upward; let's have no more talk about visions and winged souls." What might we give for a younger generation that would refuse to be made old before it even began to live and would trust its own visions!

Forty years ago, at the end of the second World War, we had a vision that we could junk all our weapons. In the intervening years we here in West Germany have spent an annual average of more than thirty billion Deutschmarks for weapons and accepted fifty million deaths from hunger in the Third World every year. This we considered the necessary price of our security. Some people said, "Stop it, this is barbaric! It is never a good rule that people should kill other people, so stop it! Let us follow a vision of peace!" They were regarded as fools and unrealistic idiots. Today we can see that our system won't work, and unfortunately we are first becoming aware of it from a financial angle. That is a rational argument, and for many people it is the only one. But perhaps the collapse of a financial system in East and West may remind us that it is also *humane* to put an end to the mad notion that we have to be able to gas, poison, or blow up every one of our fellow inhabitants of this planet two hundred times or more. Perhaps it is simply human to recall that we belong to each other. It would be a magnificent vision, and we could even live it this very moment: no more armies, no weapons, no draft, no eighteen-year-olds being taught to kill.

Humanity and open borders: This is a dream that has to come true if we want to survive. But do we learn what freedom, liberation, and happiness could be only by the blows of necessity and suffering? We ourselves are human beings; why do we have to have that drilled into us by financial compulsion? Our freedom could tell us. Our vision could give us a clear knowledge of our own nature, a magnificent idea that there was something like a self-image within us and we could follow it. No one would have the power or the ability to paint it out. We would know very clearly what we long for, what our hearts love, what we are by our very nature, and we would not allow ourselves to be deceived. We would be as certain of our goal as the swallows who fly thousands of miles from the South to the particular place where they were hatched, back to the eaves of a certain house in East Friesland. Even the best navigational instruments and the finest maps would scarcely help anyone find that spot, but a swallow knows it in its tiny head. It carries within it a very distinct picture of the place where it belongs. *That* is a vision and an inner fidelity of the heart.

In such a spirituality and religion, the old people, says Joel, will have dreams. That is also possible. There will be old people who have not stopped hoping and waiting, who have not let themselves be deceived about the meaning of their lives. Visit a retirement home. How much weariness, resignation, and unlived life do you find there! But what would it be like if the things not yet achieved were still retained as valid dreams and if one's own life, in retrospect, appeared like a dream in process of fulfillment? You only have to listen to some of them tell you what they were! They often experienced nothing but misery and hunger, war and persecution, the loss of those close to them, a chaos of suffering and pain. But even while they are telling you this, there is some glow of dignity within them. How did they survive as *human beings?* What did they believe in? How did they keep from collapsing? Where did they get the strength to take the next step into the night, on and on until daybreak? Old people with dreams. And then the generations would not forever be fighting one another and the old people would not say, "We have the truth, and we expect you to continue what we have begun; tradition is the essence of what is right." Instead, they would allow themselves to be renewed by the strength of the young. The young people in turn would not need to be rebellious and curse their elders; there could be an ongoing conversation between new departures and old wisdom, between longing and expectation, between vision and dreams from both ends of life.

You may ask, what does all that have to do with Jesus Christ? The explanation will surprise us. It is Jesus of Nazareth himself. If we listen with ears attuned to the teaching we are used to hearing, the essential will escape us. We are always ready to add the dogmatic commentary: Jesus was the Son of God, the king, the Messiah, *he* could live that way. But *we* are weak human beings, we need guidance, someone has to lead us by the hand, we are immature, we *cannot* know, we need to be led by a strong, knowledgeable, magisterial utterance from above that will protect our freedom. We need all that so that we helpless ones can be strong, always standing in the shadow of a secure, guaranteed, official leadership.

Talking about Christ that way can become a lazy excuse that diverts us from what Peter is saying here. This is the time of the early Church, which later dogmatic theology is unaware of. And here we find it word for word. It was this Jesus of Nazareth whom God made to be Christ, Messiah, and king through his resurrection. That means that Jesus of Nazareth was a human being like us. In his own lifetime he would not listen to any talk about his being a Messiah or a king, because that would only have led back to those ancient nationalistic and political falsehoods and forward to new ideologies of power. But as a human being, he risked himself so much, trusting in God, that he did not fear death and began *to live* during his own lifetime. Those who have understood this—that death has no more power, that fear is not an argument, that delay is impossible, but that we can begin to live *today*—will see what a royal human being is and what is the source of the dignity of Jesus the Messiah. Then death no longer exists, and the resurrection will show that God is true to the one who, as a human being, is committed to the truth of the divine. In the power of this Christ-king, we ourselves awaken as royal people. A few chapters later,

Peter will experience that in his own life. There are no more prison walls. Locked in, guarded by four men, and bound with chains, there he lies when the angel of the Lord comes and awakens him from the sleep of death, and he will walk through it all, and nothing will hold him back. These are the miracles that God does in heaven and on earth. We are wonderful human beings, gifted and called to accept and realize our own nature. And that is how the Church would be. *What* it is, is completely secondary; *who* we *are* when we believe in Jesus is the first, and for the moment, the only important thing. The beginning is much more crucial than the organization of the consequences, because we use those to shelter ourselves from the provocations of what is new, to keep from really starting over. We begin by beginning.

39. A Square of Sky

After this I had a vision of a great multitude, which no one could count, from every nation, race, people, and tongue. They stood before the throne and before the Lamb, wearing white robes and holding palm branches in their hands. . . .

"These are the ones who have survived the time of great distress; they have washed their robes and made them white in the blood of the Lamb.

"For this reason they stand before God's throne
and worship God day and night in God's temple.
The one who sits on the throne will shelter them.
They will not hunger or thirst anymore,
nor will the sun or any heat strike them.
For the Lamb who is in the center of the throne will
shepherd them
and lead them to springs of lifegiving water,
and God will wipe away every tear from their eyes."
                                        (Rev. 7: 9, 14b-17)

What has changed in our lives because of the message of the resurrection?

When the Church chooses the Book of Revelation to be read at the celebrations on these Sundays after Easter, it is because this change is thought to be best described in terms of a newly discovered vision of heaven. The most important change that has occurred is in the vision of that world in which we are really meant to live.

The importance of seeing the heavens open, as the visionary on Patmos did, was unintentionally attested to some years ago by a Jewish woman, Janina David. She describes her childhood in the Warsaw ghetto: her family in flight from Nazi thugs and she herself, a little child, stuffed into a tiny, dark room; no one must know that there were Jews living there. In the middle of all this fear and deprivation, there was one tiny window, and that is what she called her autobiography, *A Square of Sky.* It is possible for the world to be very dark and to offer us many reasons for sorrow and despair. None of those reasons has disappeared, and many may have become more obvious than ever, and yet there is this bit of sky in our world. It is visible, and through it there falls a bright ray of light in our darkness.

When we in the West celebrate the Eucharist, we usually do so in remembrance of Jesus' table fellowship, and we gather around the altar to put our lives at God's disposal and to receive them again, blessed. When the eastern Church celebrates the holy Eucharist, it is like an endless commentary on this bit of heaven visible since Easter morning. If you enter a church building belonging to the Byzantine or Russian Orthodox Church, you behold a wall of images. The eastern Church wants to tell us that this is already our life. We do not really see God, and everything we can say about God is spoken in images and symbols, but they are so tangibly present to us, where we can see and touch them, that the kiss of prayer can reach them. When Mass is celebrated in these churches on Sunday, it rises like a hymn that God has personally placed in our hearts, "a new song," in the words of the Book of Revelation. The Mass celebrates the resurrection of Christ, as if heaven came down to earth and we, at least for an hour or two, could share in the eternal liturgy before the throne of God, with the palm branches of victory and peace in our hands.

The Russian author Dostoyevski wrote, around 1870, that it is said the people do not know Christ because they can scarcely read or write and because the liturgy is not explained to them. I say that the people have known Christ for centuries, in all the suffering, degradation, and pain by which they have been taught the mystery of cross and resurrection. This seer on Patmos to whom we owe the last book of the Bible must have thought the same.

There is little more that we can say. These are visions that will not be suppressed, and they are written for a suffering Church. We can scarcely imagine the early Church at the end of the first century, still a tiny group and yet already caught in the machinery of persecution by Roman officialdom. Contemporary with these visions of heaven, one of the greatest Roman historians wrote three incidental sentences about the Christians. He still regarded them as a Jewish sect, and he comments that this, like all the other filth of the whole empire, had to reach Rome sooner or later. This was the time when the machinery of war was growing weary. It was brought from the battlefields of the colonies and presented live before the public in the Roman circuses, and the Christians were the welcome and unwilling supernumeraries in this drama of blood and thrills. In this inhuman era, the tiny group of those who confessed Christ never stopped believing in heaven, in the power of love in the face of hate, in the power of truth in the face of lies, and in the greatness of humanity in the face of the wretchedness of the powerful, and they were supported by the strongest conviction of all: that life cannot be killed and that in suffering they could only understand more deeply why Christ had already suffered. These were his words: You are the light of the world. You are the leaven in the mass of flour and water.

The early Church did not cease believing in its mission, in spite of all the attacks, and it was thus able to understand Christ in a new way. Wherever human beings suffer on behalf of humanity, they know in faith that Christ is at their side and that when they walk in his paths they are under his protection.

After Janina David had finished her first book, the story of her childhood in Warsaw, she wrote another. This one was called *A Square of Earth*. They belong together. The view of a world that knows no more suffering is full of consolation because of the gentleness and kindness of God, before which the burdens of heat fall away and thirst, longing, and desire are stilled. This glimpse of the true world allows us to hold out in this one.

It is only a vision of the seer on Patmos, received in the midst of want, misery, and persecution, and yet it tells us that the walls are open and the world that would otherwise be like a grave is transformed into the space of a cathedral through whose glowing windows the light of heaven falls. When our hearts are lifted in praise and adoration, the earth is transformed: It conquers pain and is open to forgiveness and capable of purity. This promise is also to be found in Revelation. They will come from all peoples and nations into a realm without borders, for it is always fear, and nothing but fear, that establishes boundaries, that fences off and ties down. But God's truth is like a breath of wind that carries the seeds of life throughout the whole world.

40. Heaven Is Open

Then I saw a new heaven and a new earth. The former heaven and the former earth had passed away, and the sea was no more. I also saw the holy city, a new Jerusalem, coming down out of heaven from God, prepared as a bride adorned for her husband. I heard a loud voice from the throne saying, "Behold, God's dwelling is with the human race. He will dwell with them and they will be his people and God himself will always be with them [as their God]. He will wipe every tear from their eyes, and there shall be no more death or mourning, wailing or pain, [for] the old order has passed away." The one who sat on the throne said, "Behold, I make all things new" (Rev. 21:1-5a).

It may be that the words of the Book of Revelation about an open heaven have never had such a powerful influence on human beings as they did at the beginning of the past century in the hearts of African slaves in the southern United States. They had been robbed of their homes, and in the ocean crossing half or more than half of them died of hunger and sickness. They were sold between the tobacco and the bananas to the highest bidder, for twenty or thirty dollars. They wore iron fetters and were beaten at their owners' pleasure. Even the number of their children was fixed and accounted for. They had nothing of their own, and more than anything, they were deprived of the right to their own humanity. That was their earthly fate: backs bent in the cotton fields, weary limbs in the evening, an unbearable life—had it not been for the message brought by the Methodist preachers who gave these slaves a dream of heaven, a faith without any hope for this world. In the souls of these people, the Book of Revelation and the visions of an open heaven became melancholy, magnificent hymns, songs of the spirit: "Lay down your load beside Jordan," "Some day I'll walk the golden streets," "I will see my father and mother," "Swing low, sweet chariot," and others without end, the dreams of longing.

Today, one hundred fifty years later, we have gotten used to regarding dreams of heaven as dangerous and even somewhat treacherous. It is not right to make misery and slavery bearable by offering fantasies of another world, and the voice from heaven tells us to fight against injustice. The images of the beyond are symbols of real life, and it must begin here and now; they do not offer consolation, but encouragement, engagement, and the spirit of combat.

That is certainly true, one might think. It is impossible to talk about heaven and leave the earth a hell. But what can we promise in this world?

The Book of Revelation offers us a picture of martyrs who had washed their garments white in the blood of the Lamb. Is it really possible to recapture innocence through suffering and pain? The idea that there must be another life beyond this one first arose among the Jews—the most historically conscious people that ever lived—in connection with martyrs, people who dared to tell their own times what they believed and what they thought was true, no matter what might become of them. It represented a break with confidence in history, at least on the individual level. It doesn't add up to say that the logic of world history is itself the judgment of the world and is governed by God's providence. Far from it. The best are often wasted and crushed, and no one knows what good can come of it.

Drive your car from Paderborn to Hamburg and you cannot avoid passing the sign pointing to Bergen-Belsen. There, when the second World War was almost over, unknown tens of thousands of people died meaningless deaths, and it is certain that among them were thousands who died because they had dared to say the right thing at the right time. We don't even know their names or what they said; it is all swept away by the wind and scattered like ashes. That is the way it is with human history. It is not true that the greatness of our spirit will be preserved in the memories of those who come after us. There were others who wrote and preached their resistance, and we remember them, but did they accomplish anything? The events of the time may have gone on in spite of them, and often people only later realized the truth of what they wanted and what they said. But that kind of learning from mistakes is surely not what one could call effectiveness!

Perhaps still poorer are those who must watch time passing them by. Alexander Solzhenitsyn, for example, called inhumanity by its name in *The Gulag Archipelago,* but at an inopportune time. He was right, and he got more than he wanted. He was uprooted and sent into exile and had to observe that everything he had said came only a few years too early. Today the sparrows are chirping it from the rooftops and people are putting up monuments to the victims of Stalinism. But it is all passing Solzhenitsyn by. He is becoming a bitter old man. He is unable to write any more. Everything he said in Russian made no sense in America, and standing between the fronts, having no home anywhere, and going on living when one is already dead is a modern form of martyrdom. History does not stop, certainly not for those who take it seriously.

So it is good to know that there are visions of a very different world. We need to tell them to people who have lost faith in their own lives, and sometimes we have to believe them without saying anything at all. If we did not have this hope, would we have the courage to endure? As long as we think that we have something to do and accomplish within history, we have to think in long stretches of time, be politically wise, plan pragmatically, weigh what we say. But the words fail us. In the end we are so wise that we lose all our courage. Heaven is not a symbol of our real lives; it is the reason why we should finally begin *today* to do and say what we feel and think. History stretches out for millennia, but heaven teaches us to live *today.* For that very reason, we need that other life, that secret vision, so that we will have the courage to dare. This prospect is the reason we can be confident and strong, patient and ready to risk. Even if we look beyond history, we have in this earthly existence so much suffering to which there is no answer, so much sickness, age, and want that we cannot change, no matter what the social structures, no matter what good means we apply. We see people who have grown so weary that they scarcely even want to imagine another life; they cling desperately to this earth, beaten down and without hope. Often what we must do is to hope on their behalf against all appearances and remember that the hands of God are spread over the life of every human being, no matter how empty and vacant it has become, and those hands are there to protect it and lead it back to the springs of water. Everything we know of heaven is taken from our own world, and to imagine it rightly we erase the limitations of the earthly and put a negation before everything: Heaven will be a place where there are no more tears. Heaven will be a place where burning heat no longer troubles people. Heaven will be a place where there is no more lamentation or pain. Heaven is a life without all the narrow walls that here hold us imprisoned as in a dungeon. Otherwise we know nothing except this: It is necessary to hope beyond all imagining and to believe in this world. It is great because it is a preparation. It has value and dignity because it is a transition and our little human lives are like a sowing of stars thrown into endless space. On the journey, we are great.

Fifth Sunday
after Easter

41. How Can We Know the Way?

"Do not let your hearts be troubled. You have faith in God; have faith also in me. In my Father's house there are many dwelling places. If there were not, would I have told you that I am going to prepare a place for you? And if I go and prepare a place for you, I will come back again and take you to myself, so that where I am you also may be. Where [I] am going you know the way." Thomas said to him, "Master, we do not know where you are going; how can we know the way?" Jesus said to him, "I am the way and the truth and the life. No one comes to the Father except through me. If you know me, then you will also know my Father. From now on you do know him and have seen him." Philip said to him, "Master, show us the Father, and that will be enough for us." Jesus said to him, "Have I been with you for so long a time, and you still do not know me, Philip? Whoever has seen me has seen the Father. How can you say, 'Show us the Father'? Do you not believe that I am in the Father and the Father is in me? The words that I speak to you I do not speak on my own. The Father

who dwells in me is doing his works. Believe me that I am in the
Father and the Father is in me, or else, believe because of the
works themselves. Amen, amen, I say to you, whoever believes
in me will do the works that I do, and will do greater ones than
these, because I am going to the Father" (Jn 14:1-12).

Like circles on the surface of a lake, moving outward from a sinking
stone—that is the impression we receive from the words of Jesus in the
fourth Gospel. They begin at an invisible center and move outward to
the edges of the world. The words Jesus says to his disciples in this
hour of his departure are such as were never spoken on earth before.
They are words of trust and confidence that Jesus' disciples can only
receive beyond the borders of death in their experience of eternal life.
Only then, looking back, can they hear Jesus speaking words like these
in the Gospel of John. It is as if Jesus were speaking to hearers who are
not present in this moment, those who neither see the moment of death
for which Jesus is preparing nor comprehend that these words are being
spoken to soothe their anxiety. All this will be acute for them only when
it is almost too late, or just in time for a whole world to be rescued from
destruction through works that are still greater than those that were
possible in the few years that Jesus spent among us.

Everything that Jesus wanted to give his disciples for their journey
in this hour when he himself was about to set his feet on the road to
death can be summarized in a single truth: At the moment we die, we
do not enter into death, but into God, who is the Father of us all.
Therefore Jesus begins with a word of comfort: "Do not let your hearts
be troubled." These are words spoken over the abyss, for even the tiny
basis for confidence that the disciples are given will very soon be torn
from them under the pressure of violence and lies. Then all the
questions that Jesus is trying to answer here will arise again. What
really sustains us, and how can we live in such a way that our life is
not an endless dying? What is the genuine reality and truth of our
existence that makes it worthwhile to live, even in the face of all
contradiction? Jesus answers all the questions of our existence with a
word that conjures up and appeals to the substance of all his confidence. He summarizes it in one word: "Father."

No matter what individuals may associate with this word, it is clear
what Jesus intends by it. There are cultural contexts in which it is
impossible to say "father" without expressing something quite differ-

ent. If being a father only means begetting children who, as men, will assist in the fields and go to war, and as women will become goods for exchange in the market, that is not what Jesus means by "Father." If we look at folk narratives, the fathers often resemble cannibalistic ogres and sheer monsters. What Jesus means by "Father" can, however, be a great many things in the life of different individuals: friend, or brother, or sister, or uncle, or grandfather. Wherever we have experiences of trust and security, we can apply the word that Jesus used when he spoke of God. He did it in a way that was unusual in Israel, with complete familiarity and trust. Jesus wanted to express by that the fact that we should have a confidence in God in the face of all our anxieties, confidence that will make this earth and the few years we live in it a home for us, or at least a shelter on the side of the road to eternity. For that is how it is with us: We need the vision of an endless life in order *really* to live the few years of our earthly existence, and we need the image of a God in the background of our existence, a God who desires us and sustains us, if we are to dare to be human beings. Therefore the disciples are quite right when they ask, "Show us the Father." But how can that be? It is not possible simply to point to God as we might to something foreign, "objective," or independent of human beings. We can certainly speak about God as an independent being, but that is a quite different image from what Jesus wanted to show the disciples, and from the one that is the source and sustenance of our human lives.

In the mid-1950s, Reinhold Schneider wandered through the Natural History Museum in Vienna, searching in the gigantic display halls among the relics of millions of years of life for some traces of the face of God. What he found was the image of a treadmill God, the master of the endlessly revolving universe, undoubtedly wise and mighty, but infinitely far from us and offering no answer to the questions we human beings pose, icy in his greatness, indifferent in his view of things, almost hideous in his massive equilibrium. We can point to God in the background of creation, but we find no access through it to the one who could appear to us as our Father. There is only one way to show God in that form, and Jesus summarizes it in his own person. He dares to say, "Whoever sees me, sees the Father." This is true, and it remains the basis of all that we have to say to one another on this subject. Whenever we try to live in such a human way that others feel a little bit at home in their own existence, a trace of God and God's fatherly goodness is visible. Whenever we dare to live somehow in terms of what Jesus tried to bring to this world, in understanding, openness, and freedom, God will be more believable for us as the basis of our hope and confidence.

All that the disciples and those around Jesus could learn when they got involved with him happened in such moments of deeper recognition. They saw that there is a kind of trust that can heal us of sickness, untruth, and lies. It is possible to accept the life that is in us, a life that is not counterfeit. Jesus gave people courage to believe that all the chains of fear could be removed from us. Therefore John calls Jesus, in his own words, *the* truth. Otherwise we may feel hemmed in and smothered, pressured and immobilized, and our existence seems like a musty tomb filled with decay instead of a blooming life. In Jesus' company it was possible to inhale the breath of immortality and to look at the world before one's eyes, a world open and free. The fourth Gospel calls this man from whom came so much life force, in his own words, *the* life. And because he showed the way to God that enables us to be human, it also calls him *the* way.

The question is, what do we want to believe about Jesus? He never attempts to prove himself. Whenever we try to understand him, he points beyond himself to this mystery that he calls God and in whom he lives. All the power of his humanity and his goodness he traces to this center of his trust. Logically, it is a circular path. God appears as Father when we are able to live in the reconciled way Jesus showed us and lived for us in his whole being. But he received that power from God, whom he believes in as Father. It is not possible to enter this circle of trust by thinking about it from without; it can only be entered in the decision of one's own life. "If you believe," Jesus says, "you will do the same works." Such faith is not a believing-that; it is like a matter-of-fact effect of the energy that comes from Jesus, a simple continuation within the reality of our lives. None of it is cleverly thought out; we simply *cannot* do otherwise if we get involved with Jesus and begin to understand who he is. That in turn means getting a clear impression of who we ourselves are and can be. Of course, at that point an enormous bridge is stretched from this world to a very different one, for at the moment of dying, we never enter into death; we enter into God. That is the hope Jesus wanted to give us. He left us here at home in our earthly existence and set out on his journey to prepare an eternal dwelling for us. As little as is the difference between the humanity we live here and the trust in God as our Father, just as little is the difference between faith in eternal life and the human reality of our earthly existence. Both belong closely together, mutually influence each other, and represent a unified experience. We are going toward something that awaits us and does not reject us. We are not separated from one another in death. Rather, in the few years that we are in time, we precede one another in order to prepare, on the other shore, the places where we will see one another again. In the eyes of eternity, death never separates us. There is only the one realm of love, without borders, without differences, without separation.

There remains this one way that is Jesus, and that leads us through the world to the other shore. It is a way as warm and light, as the beams of the sun that shatter on the surface of the water, playing in their trembling dance and making the water light even in its depths. It is a way as light as the wind that breathes through the flowers and gives them their life and fruitfulness. It is a way as beautiful and majestic as the clouds sailing in the sky, sending their shadows and their rain on the parched earth. It is the way of our lives: "Do not let your hearts be troubled, because I am going to prepare a place for you." And "Whoever has seen me has seen the Father."

42. *Bearing Fruit*

"I am the true vine, and my Father is the vine grower. He takes away every branch in me that does not bear fruit, and everyone that does he prunes so that it bears more fruit. You are already pruned because of the word that I spoke to you. Remain in me, as I remain in you. Just as a branch cannot bear fruit on its own unless it remains on the vine, so neither can you unless you remain in me. I am the vine, you are the branches. Whoever remains in me and I in him will bear much fruit, because without me you can do nothing. Anyone who does not remain in me will be thrown out like a branch and wither; people will gather them and throw them into a fire and they will be burned. If you remain in me and my words remain in you, ask for whatever you want

and it will be done for you. By this is my Father glorified, that you bear much fruit and become my disciples. As the Father loves me, so I also love you. Remain in my love. If you keep my commandments, you will remain in my love, just as I have kept my Father's commandments and remain in his love.

"I have told you this so that my joy might be in you and your joy might be complete. This is my commandment: love one another as I love you. No one has greater love than this, to lay down one's life for one's friends. You are my friends if you do what I command you. I no longer call you slaves, because a slave does not know what his master is doing. I have called you friends, because I have told you everything I have heard from my Father. It was not you who chose me, but I who chose you and appointed you to go and bear fruit that will remain, so that whatever you ask the Father in my name he may give you" (Jn 15:1-16).

It would be possible to hear and accent the threatening undertones in this Gospel. In that case, the text would seem made to order for making people small before God, warning and frightening them. "Without me you can do nothing" would then mean God is everything, but you are little, and your existence is really nothing. Then being "thrown out" and "thrown into the fire" would mean an eternal punishment of death for every deviation. And we could go on in this way.

But undoubtedly the words of the fourth Gospel are not meant that way. It is true that God is everything and we are small, but our greatness and dignity consists in this: We are united with God, and we can be aware of that communion with God in our lives.

We human beings are, fundamentally, the only creatures on earth who can consciously sense and know that something of the current of infinity lives in them. We are the only ones who can consciously reflect that there are inclinations, abilities, and callings within us that are unique and irreplaceable and that have an absolute significance and meaning because of their origin. In union with God, our life is meant to become rich and great, and the only question is how we can remain anchored in our point of origin.

We should note with care that in the first three Gospels, Christ himself, when speaking of the relationship between God and human beings, almost always uses parables of growth, what we might call "organic" images. He does it to warn us against every kind of violence that we might exercise toward ourselves.

Everything Jesus embodies and says is so very different from the shouts of fanatical prophets and ascetic heroes. For Christ the reign of God is not something to be fought for and conquered by piling up mountains, as the Titans did, in order to storm heaven. When Christ speaks of the power of God in our lives, he likes to say: It is like a grain of mustard seed that is the tiniest of all seeds, and no one would bet a penny on its success, and yet it grows and becomes so big that the birds of the air can build their nests in it. Or it is like a farmer who has sowed seed in the field and does not know how it grows, but it does grow day by day without any help from the farmer. We should think of our relationship to God as just that unified, just that harmonious. We should let go of the fear that is always compelling us to say, "We'll take hold, we'll manage, we'll do it, and we have to do it." The only task we would have would be to let go of this desperate straining and struggling and to learn a deeper trust. In truth, everything God has to say to us is already alive in our hearts. We should not close ourselves up in fear and narrowness, but open ourselves to what really should be living in us. It is unnecessary to do any more than just stop preventing God from maturing and taking form in us.

Therefore the best interpretation of this passage from the fourth Gospel about the vine and the branches is probably found in the words of the reading from the first letter of John: "This is how we shall know that we belong to the truth and reassure our hearts before him in whatever our hearts condemn, for God is greater than our hearts and knows everything" (1 Jn 3:19-20).

It would be possible, of course, to develop these words, too, into a nightmare, the image of a God who knows everything. It can be used to make God an overseer who controls us, listens in on us, follows us, and is always on our track. But in truth this is our most important comfort and the source of our strongest confidence: When we do not know what to do, God will know. When we condemn ourselves, it is very seldom our hearts that do it. Ordinarily it is the arsenal of well-preserved prejudices in our super-ego, that almost compulsively hammers at us with the same standards, the same rules, the same orders. We are seldom capable of accusing ourselves in our hearts. And when it happens that we feel inwardly that there is a great deal in our past of which we should be ashamed, this very impression of a heart that condemns itself is often, humanly considered, the greatest thing we can see. It is really not possible to deprive someone else of this, because the reasons for the shame may truly exist. But the fact that another possesses a heart with which to condemn himself or herself is something we can highly value, and for the most part it is something we should admire. It is just that the feeling of shame should never reach the point of accusing the person's whole existence and declaring it guilty. There are also excesses of good that are not thereby better, but worse. It may appear to us that our whole life has been shredded and penetrated by every possible evil drive. When we have that feeling, we should think of these words from the first letter of John. How little we really know about our lives! How little we understand ourselves! Even when we think we can almost touch the wrong in us with our hands, rarely is the language of accusation also the language of truth.

"God knows everything," says this magnificent passage from 1 John. We must add, God knows everything—how you were formed, with what burdens you have come into being, what your childhood was like, how you grew up. Most of it is hidden from you, far from your awareness, but your Creator can make a more just judgment than you yourself. God sees not merely the things you do, but your essence, your whole self. God looks at you with kindness, because God made you out of love. God looks at you patiently, having waited an eternity for you to come into existence, and God desires that you should also learn to see yourself with kind and patient eyes. Because God knows every fiber in you and every heartbeat before you are aware of them yourself, you can trust that God will never use that knowledge against you. God only wants you to mature, gradually and slowly, in understanding yourself. For the fact that God is greater than our hearts can call us to be more open-hearted and generous to ourselves, and so to all others.

When we do that, we open ourselves more widely to the root and ground of our being, and our fruit ripens. It may happen that we will often feel ourselves to be smaller and that we are being trimmed and clipped by some other, but this pruning is a kind of gathering of power at a deeper level, the beginning of a fuller ripening. So this Gospel reading ends with a magnificent assurance: "Whatever you ask for, God will give you." It is like a promise and a hope that one day nothing will live in our hearts except what comes from God. Then all we have to pray for is that God would utter God's own self in our lives as in a prayer, and that the prayer will be answered. It is never *things* for which we pray most passionately, but fundamentally it is our right to exist and to be just as God wants us to be. God is ready to answer our prayer.

Sixth Sunday after Easter

43. Seeing from Afar

"If you love me, you will keep my commandments. And I will ask the Father, and he will give you another Advocate to be with you always, the Spirit of Truth, which the world cannot accept, because it neither sees nor knows it. But you know it, because it remains with you, and will be in you. I will not leave you orphans; I will come to you. In a little while the world will no longer see me, but you will see me, because I live and you will live. On that day you will realize that I am in my Father and you are in me and I in you. Whoever has my commandments and observes them is the one who loves me. And whoever loves me will be loved by my Father, and I will love him and reveal myself to him." Judas, not the Iscariot, said to him, "Master, [then] what happened that you will reveal yourself to us and not to the world?" Jesus answered and said to him, "Whoever loves me will keep my word, and my Father will love him, and we will come to him and make our dwelling with him. Whoever does not love me does not keep my words; yet the word you hear is not mine but that of the Father who sent me" (Jn 14:15-24).

Sometimes the places surrounding a sacred legend can offer the most impressive interpretation of the story and best help us to understand it. There is such a legend that tells how John the Evangelist, accompanied by the mother of Jesus, settled in a place near Ephesus, in present Turkey, to spend the last years of his life. The Turks call this site, now a goal of Christian pilgrims, Panayia Kapulu, "the place of the most holy." It seems well suited to explaining the calm and stately worldview of the Fourth Evangelist. Here a mountain rises above the ruins of the former world metropolis of Ephesus. The revered spot is a tiny house. In ascending this mountain where the Fourth Evangelist dwelt, one withdraws from the plain where, in its time, the great city of Ephesus carried on its wheeling and dealing, apparently enslaved to money and fame, religion and riches. One leaves the place of pulsing life and enters, step by step, into solitude. The noise of the world falls away, giving place to the shrill chirping of the cicadas, the cries of the swallows in the sky, and the light whispering of the wind in the leaves of the pine, olive, and fig trees. All our questions return: What did, or rather what does, the figure and the message of Jesus of Nazareth mean?

Looking down from the venerated mountain, one has the feeling that time and history have vanished, and one enters into an eternal answer, a knowledge above the forces of history and the world. For that is the first insight we gain: One must distance oneself widely from the things that are important to the quite normal, secure, and rational workings and works of the world. In their eyes it seemed that, only a few years after the appearance of the man from Nazareth, everything was going on as usual; it seemed that the message of Jesus of Nazareth was no longer receiving any attention or acceptance. What was the meaning of this man's death? John attempts, in the farewell discourses, to interpret and assemble the things that were literally his legacy and his dearest and most holy memorial: life itself. One thing seemed quite clear to him: With the eyes of the world, one can never understand Jesus. For it, he is as dead as if he had never lived, or as if he had come and gone without a trace.

One needs very different eyes to see what he not only gave to a whole world but would continue to give in the future, because he is the only truly Living One. That was John's conviction, and the condition for understanding the things he spoke about is a very intimate feeling of love concentrated on the person of this man from Nazareth. In the eyes of the Fourth Evangelist, Jesus is the one person who deserves to be loved absolutely, so that it is only possible to speak about him in absolutes, with a deep conviction that will never leave us.

Why does Jesus deserve to be loved in this way? The first three evangelists tell us how Jesus may have spoken while he was among us. John does not do that, saying to himself: Everything we can tell about Jesus, such as his way of speaking, will remain external to us; we would only be repeating things that could be put down in writing and would merely touch our bodily eyes. We have to talk about Jesus in such a way that he himself emerges from our hearts and is transformed into the language of love. There is talk of the commandments, and all of us know the Sermon on the Mount, with its magnificent commands even to approach our enemies in love, to pray for our persecutors, and not to withdraw in fear from death or from other people or from the day to come. John does not include a single one of these words in his Gospel. He reduces or concentrates everything in one single point. *This* is what Jesus said and desired, and everything else is only commentary: "Love one another." Because he gave us that power, says John, he is deserving of all the love of which we are capable. He made us sisters and brothers. He made us able to believe in the feeling that possesses us most deeply. It is not necessary to understand anything else of what Jesus said or commanded, because only this feeling for him is utterly strong and sustaining. All the words he said or could have said or must have said will come to us from within, as if they were our own.

Jesus' words of farewell in this Gospel passage begin, "If you love me, you will keep my commandments." That means that for those who love there are no orders from without, because they have an internal standard in their own hearts. It gets to the point that in this Gospel one's whole relationship to Jesus becomes internal and purely spiritual. In his own time there were attempts to imitate Jesus in externals, and they continue today. People have tried to imitate his style of life, even his clothing, his appearance, and his behavior. These are only copies. Jesus has been celebrated in formal language according to the religious styles of every age, and sacred spaces and churches have been built for him. But the only thing that matters is the immediacy of the heart, a feeling of pure love. Then what Jesus was and said is not past, but present, and everything speaks to us from deep within. What he said becomes our dearest possession, what he was is our own life, and then one cannot speak of Jesus as a historical person, but as a power that floods us, utterly invisible but strong as the air we breathe and the light whose warmth we feel and the twinkling of the stars that lights us in the darkness. "Spirit" is the word we use for this, because we have no other. We can describe it as a strong feeling that we can totally and deeply sense and see what it is that makes us alive. We can even turn it around, so that in everything of which we are completely sure, to the point that when we say "this is what is true for us, it makes us real and gives us the courage to live," we sooner or later find we are touching the lips of the man of Nazareth, and the words we so deeply understand are his own.

The Protestant author Jochen Klepper said more than sixty years ago that when he was on the brink of despair, he had spent the whole year doing nothing but trying to understand two or three words of the Bible. That must be what it means when Jesus here promises us that he will give his Spirit to those who love him and the Spirit will lead us to all truth. The world will not understand, but we will comprehend that we are not being left orphans. We will be close to the power to which we owe our being—God—and it is an intimate relationship in which we sense how right Jesus was when he called on us to trust in nothing but love. Jesus was in God, and we will sense this to the extent that we ourselves enter into the person of Jesus of Nazareth and abide in him. But we will also sense that he forms and penetrates our very lives.

We only need to understand a little of Jesus' message to know that all the old conflicts, eruptions, renewals, struggles and triumphs, anxieties and victories will return. It is like grasping a fish net with our hands and pulling it out of the water. No matter where we take hold, we will draw the whole net after us. It is just the same with Jesus' message. No matter where your life comes in contact with him, you will be led into the whole truth. Something of his Spirit will be alive in you, and you will sense that he was from God to the extent that he acquires reality within you. There really is such a miracle: that one human being can be for another something like the living Christ, and embody a power that is stronger than death and transcends despair. If you ask how that can be, the answer is only this one impoverished word: love. We can turn it around and say, "The one who keeps Jesus' commandments is the one who really loves," but this must not be an external thing. It must come totally from within, just as a living form acquires its structure and emerges and declares itself in its own free development. There is no more compulsion and prescription: love makes its own order, and it is precisely the same as the one that existed in Jesus' eyes. Remarkably enough, we Christians fear scarcely any energy more than the one that we call God. It seems that it is love itself that arouses the most fear within us, so that we circle around it, asking, how much are we allowed to touch each other, how much are we allowed to feel close to one another, in which parts of our bodies are we permitted to feel anything, when do we pass the limits of decency and morality? When will we have the courage, for once, to be nothing more than spirit and love? Then there would be no more contradictions between sensuality and morality, nature and culture, instinct and order, and we would simply be human beings.

If we look down from Panayia Kapulu on the ruins of Ephesus, we see the world apparently unchanged. It revolves around power, money, passions, and so many other things that cause it misery and suffering, and the message of Jesus is almost too timid to be heard in the streets and alleys of the great cities of the world. If Jesus had preached war on behalf of the oppressed, he would have been understood. If he had preached the massing of capital on behalf of the rich, he would have been understood. If he had revolted against exploitation, he would have had people behind him, and if he had been on the side of the exploiters, he would also have had a party of supporters. But to go forward in love alone, as if through walls, in all vulnerability, and to hope that there would be people who would prefer that above all, and that there is a language as soft as the wind, completely from the Spirit, that brings forth life: that is Jesus as the Fourth Evangelist paints him. He can have Jesus say, only a few sentences before today's Gospel, "I am going to prepare a place for you." Now he says the apparent opposite: "My Father and I will come and make our dwelling with you," and there is no heaven and earth, only people who are on their way to God because they already have God in themselves.

The two things augment each other. The more we enter into the eternal dwelling, the more the image of God that Jesus gave us takes on shape and permanence in us, a marvelous, sacred image, the home of the divine that is particular to each one of us. We are not orphans, but people who are sheltered and given a home in the Spirit, people who love and are therefore mediators between heaven and earth, between the stars and the dust of the streets, the highest and the lowest, gold and filth. We are people who live in tension between heaven and earth, loving in our longing and filled with happiness, on the way to an eternal home while we ourselves are already dwellings of eternity. We take one another by the hand and there are no more boundaries of death, fear, sin, or difference, perhaps not even the Johannine difference between the believers and the "world," for we have overcome the world in our own hearts and there is nothing more, only a single, concentrated light of holiness.

Sometimes we need the words of a legend to provide a place in which we can understand the words of an evangelist. We have to go up on a high mountain so that we can find our way down into the dust of the streets, and our eyes have to be opened so that we can really see.